NAVIGATING ACADEMIA AS A NEURODIVERGENT ACADEMIC

"I have read much academic writing about inclusion. This book is something else. It is raw, theoretically sharp, and genuinely moving – sometimes all three on the same page. The authors span career stages, continents, and neurotypes, yet common threads of masking, burnout, and institutional betrayal surface again and again, making the structural argument impossible to ignore. What stays with me most is the courage of contributors who refused to write the expected "over-coming" or "survival-against-the-odds" narrative and instead told the truth about where they are right now. Every academic – neurodivergent or not – should read this book."

—*Professor Angharad E. Beckett*,
Centre for Disability Studies, University of Leeds

"This groundbreaking volume unites a global community of scholars – including voices from Taiwan, Zimbabwe, and Australia – to document academic trajectories ranging from doctoral study to senior leadership. It showcases a vast spectrum of neurodivergent experiences, including Autism, ADHD, Dyslexia, Tourette's, and Sensory Processing Sensitivity, while centering the intersectional identities of trans and Global Majority researchers. Ultimately, these narratives offer an urgent manifesto for transforming the academy into a space of collective belonging by replacing ableist metrics with a genuine culture of care that celebrates neurodiversity."

—*Heng-hao Chang*, **Department of Sociology,
National Taipei University, Taiwan**

"An important and timely book that centres lived experience, challenges deficit narratives, and offers a deeply human account of what it means to be neurodivergent within modern academia. This work will resonate far beyond universities."

—*Katie Koullas*, **CEO, Yellow Ladybugs**

Series Editor: Marian Mahat, The University of Melbourne, Australia

Surviving and Thriving in Academia provides short, accessible books for navigating the many challenges, responsibilities and opportunities of academic careers. The series is particularly dedicated to supporting the professional journeys of early and mid-career academics and doctoral students, but will present books of use to scholars at all stages in their careers. Books within the series draw on real-life examples from international scholars, offering practical advice and a supportive and encouraging tone throughout.

PUBLISHED TITLES

Achieving Academic Promotion
Edited by Marian Mahat and Jennifer Tatebe

Getting the Most Out of Your Doctorate: The Importance of Supervision, Networking, and Becoming a Global Academic
Edited by Mollie Dollinger

Coaching and Mentoring for Academic Development
By Kay Guccione and Steve Hutchinson

Women Thriving in Academia
Edited by Marian Mahat

Academic Resilience: Personal Stories and Lessons Learnt from the COVID-19 Experience
Edited by Marian Mahat, Joanne Blannin, Caroline Cohrssen, and Elizer Jay de los Reyes

Academic Mobility and International Academics: Challenges and Opportunities
Edited by Jasvir Kaur Nachatar Singh

The Impactful Academic: Building a Research Career That Makes a Difference
Edited by Wade Kelly

Thriving in Academic Leadership
Edited by Sharmila Pixy Ferris and Kathleen Waldron

Supervising Doctoral Candidates
Edited by Chris Rolph

Building Communities in Academia
Edited by Melina Aarnikoivu and Ai Tam Le

Nurturing Wellbeing in Academia: How to Prioritise Your Mental Health
By Poppy Gibson

Doctoral Study and Getting Published: Narratives of Early Career Researchers
Edited by Richard Fay and Achilleas Kostoulas

Conceptualising the Academic Self: Beyond Traditional Practices
Edited by Victoria I. Ekpo and David Allan

NAVIGATING ACADEMIA AS A NEURODIVERGENT ACADEMIC

Stories of Breaking and Rebuilding

EDITED BY

SARAH TIMPERLEY
The University of Melbourne, Australia

MATTHEW HARRISON
The University of Melbourne, Australia

And

JESSICA RIORDAN
The University of Melbourne, Australia

emerald
PUBLISHING

United Kingdom – North America – Japan
India – Malaysia – China

Emerald Publishing Limited
Emerald Publishing, Floor 5, Northspring, 21-23 Wellington Street, Leeds
LS1 4DL

First edition 2026

British Library Cataloguing in Publication Data
A catalogue record for this book is available from the British Library

ISBN: 978-1-83662-557-5 (Print Hardback)
ISBN: 978-1-83662-559-9 (Print Paperback)
ISBN: 978-1-83662-556-8 (Online)
ISBN: 978-1-83662-558-2 (Epub)

CONTENTS

LIST OF FIGURES

Chapter 9

Chapter 10

FOREWORD

Steven Kapp, University of Portsmouth

This foreword comes with a backstory that I declined to write an invited chapter on imposter syndrome, recommending Jenny Phan instead on the basis of her exceptional advice on the topic and success as a neurodivergent academic, activist woman of Asian descent (Phan, 2025).[1]

I battle imposter syndrome too deeply to feel worthy of imparting advice, because I don't feel that I meet the metrics to be considered a successful academic (at least by traditional academic standards). Rather than – in the words of one of the assessors of the UK's Research Excellence Framework – 'building a castle' through one's progressive line of research to generate impact, I prefer to stand on the shoulder of giant collaborators to help lay bricks so that others can build their castles.

Fortunate to have met my neurodiversity and disability rights movement mentor Scott Michael Robertson as an undergraduate by chance (he reached out to me after a Facebook post) in February 2007 months after he co-founded the Autistic Self Advocacy Network, I have been trying to help merge science or research and advocacy through research on and inspired by the movements. In parallel, I have tried to help raise the profile and contributions of neurodivergent academics and co-researchers through participatory research. Disinterested in hierarchy like many autistic and neurodivergent academics[2], I have followed Jones's past advice of being careful before asking for promotion (Jones, 2023). As authors attest, our labours of care, purpose and passion may help

[1] See also the chapter *Imposter Syndrome as a Neurodivergent Early Career Academic.*
[2] See the chapter *It Doesn't Get Any Easier at the Top (At Least Not Yet).*

us to influence the field, but often at our own expense. For me, 'success' meant giving up nearby family support and a lifelong entitlement to developmental services for 'substantial support needs'[3] (subsequently having to rely on private funding for support) to simultaneously have my first (1) full-time, career-track job; (2) independent living (beyond on campus with an unlimited meal plan) and (3) residence beyond a 10-mile radius to literally become a foreigner 'across the pond'.

To my knowledge, I have the most citations of any openly autistic autism academic in the field. However, as I appear to embody the establishment as a white, straight, cisgender male from the US working (and 'naturalised') in the United kingdom, I do not wish to take up too much space. Instead, I wish to centre the voices of a broad diversity of neurodivergent people. Indeed, the book abounds with lived experience of intersectionality foreign to me. So I have turned down or not sought opportunities such as contributing to a roundtable on autistic academics (while co-organising it from behind on the editorial board: Dwyer et al., 2021), not spoken at the ITAKOM conference (but my recruitment there of potential students for the disability studies-related Master's I teach on may have saved the course that summer), and did not co-edit a special issue on autism and the social model (but we managed to publish in it an important paper I helped to plan beginning in my PhD: Dwyer et al., 2025). Examples of laying bricks for others – although they also do make their own way – include co-founding the International Society of Autism Research's Autistic Researchers Committee and supporting T.C. Waisman and Patrick Dwyer to lead it, then declining and successfully suggesting Patrick when asked to join the Membership Committee. I have seen Patrick build castles with bridges across divides in the autism community,

[3] After being diagnosed as autistic at age 13, I had a re-diagnosis of autism with Level 2 support needs (despite my misgivings over the term: Kapp & Ne'eman, 2020; Kapp, 2023) that granted me access to California's regional centre services on appeal. These services are for people with developmental disabilities, specifically with intellectual disability or equivalent impairment, and helped me access support in the self-direction, daily living, and employability domains. Paradoxically at 5 a.m. on the morning of the appeal, I submitted my dissertation proposal, but the inability to better manage my time was just a slice of my disability.

helping to authoritatively bring critical ideas to more traditional audiences and disciplines (Dwyer, 2022).

I am also wary of susceptibility to my – like many neurodivergent academics'[4] – tendency to overcommit. Looking back, the intensity of work on my book (Kapp & Ne'eman, 2020) inadvertently sacrificed a relationship, absorbing nights and weekends (at a time when my visa was expiring and my partner needed reassurance of stability). Like many of us, I have struggled to set boundaries in my working life[5], and not having a family and the complexities they entail[6] has sometimes left poor self-care practices with less resistance[7]. I know our health may suffer when apparent security such as 'permanent' contracts begins to lose meaning, which we must protect further at time of rising 'anti-intellectualism'[8]. I have the paradoxical 'accommodation' of being able to come into the office whenever I want (accommodating sensory needs), which I am using on an extended deadline as I finish this draft ahead of a meeting at midnight (applying self-pressure[9]). I hope that my example helps instil more confidence in neurodivergent scholars to push boundaries, in the field and against their own self-doubt.

TOWARDS NEURODIVERSE FUTURES IN ACADEMIA

Our neurodivergences that lead us to defy (whether consciously or by default) academic norms and deploy strengths can change academia through leadership[10]. As noted in the opening chapter, authors and editors have faced many obstacles, sometimes at great personal detriment. Indeed, as I have helped to demonstrate,

[4] See the chapter *Burnout in Environments Shaped By Scarcity.*
[5] See the chapter *It Doesn't Get Any Easier at the Top (At Least Not Yet).*
[6] See the chapters *Between Research and Resistance: Insights From a Trans Neurodivergent PhD Student* and *Navigating Unexpected Detours During the Transition From Student to Academic Career.*
[7] I have a hospitalisation caused by skin infection in reaction to eye shadow glitter to celebrate my then-new #slaydhd diagnosis to show for it.
[8] See the chapter *Burnout in Environments Shaped by Scarcity.*
[9] See the chapter *Becoming a Sensitive Scholar: Navigating the Academic Assemblages in East Asia.*
[10] See the chapter *It Doesn't Get Any Easier at the Top (At Least Not Yet).*

neurodivergent strengths often pose challenges that depend on context (Russell et al., 2019).

Divergent thinking, pattern-detection and hyperfocus led me to 'quadruple down' – I cannot remember each of the three other steps – into turning a disagreement with an advisor into my dissertation. 'Pre-dissertation'-inspired concepts have finally found their way into the literature, organised by special collections and invitations that provide structure through deadlines (Kapp, 2018; Kapp et al., 2019; Kapp, 2023; Kapp, 2025; Kapp & Gudknecht, 2025; Kapp, n.d.). We often pursue 'side quests' that enhance our careers and academia[11], such as the first paper to my knowledge to (1) directly compare autistic and non-autistic people's views on autism (on the same measure), (2) quantitatively examine autistic people's views on autism and to directly compare (affirmatively) people with formally diagnosed and self-identified autism (Kapp et al., 2013). This paper helped me get headhunted to come to the United Kingdom, made in part possible by an academic who gave me the opportunity to co-lead it (Gillespie-Lynch).

Our fear of failure may sometimes drive us to dig in further where others would avoid (South et al., 2011), such as responding to the epidemic injustice of being said to be biased as a neurodivergent academic (as though neuronormative academics achieve objectivity: Botha, 2021) through incorporating overwhelming patterns of empirical evidence in research (Kapp, 2025) and advocacy (Kapp & Ne'eman, 2012).

Neurodivergent mentorship can help pave the way forward. (Although I caution that I have observed neurodivergent academics with limited power perpetuate oppressive systems because of ideological agreement or deference to authority.) With our exceptionally 'spiky profiles' or uneven cognitive skills (Jones et al., 2009), we thrive when we have supportive environments. I have supported neurodivergent PhD students even where it caused conflict with colleagues (e.g. Munday), or where they decide to leave academia to affect policy more directly.

[11] See the chapter *People, Politics, Power Structures, and Politeness: a Crash Course in Social Dynamics I Would Rather Have Avoided.*

Mentorship comes with the perceived responsibility to tirelessly advocate for your mentees, both in academia and in broader systems that have failed them. In turn, it also comes with mentees who care about you. A couple of neurodivergent PhD students have half-jokingly warned I might die if I did not take leave. We need to support one another, at a time when it seems too easy to feel bleak about the future of academia and society. Hope remains: growing up in the heart of autism's medical model in Southern California and studying in it at UCLA, I have used my privilege as an openly autistic researcher alongside other activists or academics to influence the autism diagnosis itself (Kapp & Ne'eman, 2020), and promote a world where more neurodivergent people feel comfortable stepping into their identities and power (Ahuvia et al., 2026).

We are all laying bricks, and need a whole community to turn those bricks into a castle with defences strong enough to fortify against the threats to research, universities, any semblance of work–life balance and freedom. Metaphors for these times may feel dark, but I have seen certain literally menacing portrayals of neurodivergence such as Autism Speaks' *I Am Autism* retreat. At the start of our PhDs, ASAN's LA/UCLA Chapter Co-Chair Sarah Pripas-Kapit and I met with Autism Speaks' executive director of the local chapter to clearly express the autistic community's concerns, which he respected and said he would relay the message to the national organisation. It, the most powerful autism advocacy organisation (certainly at the time), took down the video shortly thereafter and has arguably never since had any representation nearly so based in fear or pity. It is important though that changes sweep far beyond media representation and language (Robinson, 2020; Rosenblatt, 2018) to every aspect of society (Chapman, 2024; Kapp, 2024). The stories in this book illustrate how important it is that academic institutions make changes so that neurodivergent academics can attain our achievements *without* harm caused by burnout and imposer syndrome.

REFERENCES

Ahuvia, I. L., Gurbuz, E., Cuda, J., Kapp, S. K., Houck, A., Gates, J. A., Schleider, J. L., & Gurba, A. N. (2026). Identifying as autistic without a formal diagnosis: Who self-identifies as autistic and why? *Autism in Adulthood*, 25739581251409920.

Botha, M. (2021). Academic, activist, or advocate? Angry, entangled, and emerging: A critical reflection on autism knowledge production. *Frontiers in Psychology*, *12*, 727542.

Chapman, R. (2024). Toward neurodivergent power. *Boston Review*.

Dwyer, P. (2022). The neurodiversity approach(es): What are they and what do they mean for researchers? *Human Development*, *66*(2), 73–92. https://www.jstor.org/stable/27139651

Dwyer, P., Acevedo, S. M., Brown, H. M., Grapel, J., Jones, S. C., Nachman, B. R., Raymaker, D. M., & Williams, Z. J. (2021). An expert roundtable discussion on experiences of autistic autism researchers. *Autism in Adulthood*, *3*(3), 209–220.

Dwyer, P., Gurba, A. N., Kapp, S. K., Kilgallon, E., Hersh, L. H., Chang, D. S., & Gillespie-Lynch, K. (2025). Community views of neurodiversity, models of disability and autism intervention: Mixed methods reveal shared goals and key tensions. *Autism*, *29*(9), 2297–2314.

Jones, C. R., Happé, F., Golden, H., Marsden, A. J., Tregay, J., Simonoff, E., & Charman, T. (2009). Reading and arithmetic in adolescents with autism spectrum disorders: Peaks and dips in attainment. *Neuropsychology*, *23*(6), 718–728.

Jones, S. C. (2023). Advice for autistic people considering a career in academia. *Autism*, *27*(7), 2187-2192.

Kapp, S., & Ne'eman, A. (2012). *ASD in DSM-5: What the research shows and recommendations for change*. Autistic Self Advocacy Network.

Kapp, S. K. (2018). Social support, well-being, and quality of life among individuals on the autism spectrum. *Pediatrics*, *141*(Suppl. 4), S362–S368.

Kapp, S. K. (2023). Profound concerns about "profound autism": Dangers of severity scales and functioning labels for support needs. *Education Sciences*, *13*(2), 106.

Kapp, S. K. (2024). More than modest proposals. *Boston Review*.

Kapp, S. K. (2025). Sensory–movement underpinnings of lifelong neurodivergence: Getting a grip on autism. *Frontiers in Integrative Neuroscience*, *19*, 1489322.

Kapp, S. K., Gillespie-Lynch, K., Sherman, L. E., & Hutman, T. (2013). Deficit, difference, or both? Autism and neurodiversity. *Developmental Psychology*, *49*(1), 59-71.

Kapp, S. K., Goldknopf, E., Brooks, P. J., Kofner, B., & Hossain, M. (2019). Expanding the critique of the social motivation theory of autism with participatory and developmental research. *Behavioral and Brain Sciences*, *42*, e94.

Kapp, S. K., & Gudknecht, J. (2025). The strengths of speech divergence in autistic people: Implications for assessment and support. *Infant and Child Development*, *34*(3), e70017.

Kapp, S. K., & Ne'eman, A. (2020). Lobbying autism's diagnostic revision in the DSM-5. In S. K. Kapp (Ed.). *Autistic community and the neurodiversity movement: Stories from the frontline* (pp. 167–194).

Kapp, S. K. (n.d., in press). The neurodiversity movement vs. the medical model of autism. *World Psychiatry*.

Phan, J. M. (2025). Navigating neurotypical norms in academic research: A perspective from an autistic early career researcher. *Autism in Adulthood*, *7*(2), 133–140. https://doi.org/10.1089/aut.2023.0182

Robison, J. E. (2020). My time with autism speaks. *Autistic community and the neurodiversity movement*, 221–241.

Rosenblatt, A. (2018). Autism, advocacy organizations, and past injustice. *Disability Studies Quarterly*, *38*(4). https://doi.org/10.18061/dsq.v38i4.6222

Russell, G., Kapp, S. K., Elliott, D., Elphick, C., Gwernan-Jones, R., & Owens, C. (2019). Mapping the autistic advantage from the accounts of adults diagnosed with autism: A qualitative study. *Autism in Adulthood*, *1*(2). 124–133. https://doi.org/10.1089/aut.2018.0035

South, M., Dana, J., White, S. E., & Crowley, M. J. (2011). Failure is not an option: Risk-taking is moderated by anxiety and also by cognitive ability in children and adolescents diagnosed with an autism spectrum disorder. *Journal of Autism and Developmental Disorders*, *41*(1), 55-65.

ACKNOWLEDGEMENTS

First and foremost, we would like to acknowledge all of the wonderful authors who contributed to this work. We were truly touched by how generous each of you were to share your stories, expertise and enthusiasm throughout this process. Thank you for making early and late meetings across conflicting time zones and figuring out what this book would be together.

We would also like to acknowledge the authors who planned to contribute but were unable to because the world sometimes throws too much at us to handle all at once. The insights, stories and kind words you shared are still cherished. Even if they did not make it into these pages, they have left their mark on our thinking.

Thank you to our global neurodivergent community for showing us we're not alone and giving us the strength to be open as ourselves. Thank you to both those blazing a trail as openly neurodivergent people and to those who work quietly behind the scenes to improve things even in spaces that feel hostile. We know it's not safe for everyone to be out, but your neurodivergent family around the world still see and appreciate you.

Thank you to the wonderful artists who contributed to this book, Melissa Vallence, Abby Lastowski and Olivia Dang.

Finally, we would like to acknowledge the Wurundjeri Woiwurrung peoples as traditional owners of the unceded land where we lived and worked during the editing of this book.

Sarah, Matthew and Jessica

I would like to thank my partner, Ana. You make me feel like existing in the ways I need to exist is not just okay but encouraged. You constantly inspire me to keep figuring out who I want to be.

I would also like to thank my grandma (or Damma as she's known in our family). I know I don't ask for advice often, because

I'm terrible at asking for advice. But when I do, you're my first port of call. I honestly love your mixture of encouragement, cynicism and bluntness. Never change.

Sarah

Life can sometimes be chaotic, especially when living with me, so I would like to thank my partner Sarah (different Sarah!), my parents and friends for embracing my quirks, and our broader University of Melbourne community for their support. A special thank you to my mentor and sponsor for all of these years, Professor Lorraine Graham, who begins retirement the very day that we submitted the manuscript for this book. Lorraine did what she does best, and generously reviewed Chapter 1 and provided sage advice throughout the writing process. Finally, I would be remiss not to celebrate the collective achievements of the global neurodiversity movement in creating a more inclusive world – this will be a long journey, but it is a privilege to travel alongside you as we all do the work that needs to be done.

Matt

First, I would just like to say a huge thank you to my co-editors and close friends, Matt and Sarah, and my husband Ben for keeping me afloat during the last six months while I navigated unexpected and serious health challenges. Your care, steadiness and endless generosity sustained me without question when my capacity was limited and my spirits low, making it possible for me to keep moving forward.

Finally, for my daughters, Amelia and Matilda, who helped me find myself all those years ago when I didn't even know I was lost. Through sleepless nights, endless movement, big feelings and fierce advocacy, you continue to teach me what really matters. This work, and the roads that are built from it, are for you.

Jess

1

LOCATING OURSELVES IN THE MODERN ACADEMY

SARAH TIMPERLEY, MATTHEW HARRISON AND JESSICA RIORDAN

The University of Melbourne, Australia

ABSTRACT

This introductory chapter situates the book within the contemporary academy and explains why this collection is both necessary and timely. It outlines how neurodivergent academics are navigating institutions that increasingly claim inclusion while operating through systems that intensify pressure, precarity and exclusion. Rather than rehearsing the history of the neurodiversity movement, this chapter frames the book as a collective act of sense-making, grounded in first-person storytelling across career stages, disciplines and global contexts. It introduces shared concepts that recur throughout the volume, including the double empathy problem, masking, and autistic burnout, as relational and systemic experiences shaped by neurotypically structured environments. Alongside harm and marginalisation, the chapter foregrounds community, creativity and moments of belonging. Written for neurodivergent academics and for colleagues seeking deeper understanding, this opening chapter sets the tone for an honest, critical and compassionate exploration of academic life.

Keywords: Neurodiversity; higher education; inclusion; academia; lived experience; masking; burnout; double empathy

Source: Artwork by Melissa Vallence.
A Depiction of Our Place in the Modern University.

WHY THIS BOOK AND WHY NOW?

Academia is experiencing (and has been for some time) a reckoning: a growing recognition of how its systems cause harm to disabled and neurodivergent staff and students, alongside increased calls for inclusion (Mellifont, 2023; Tan et al., 2024). This book does not aim to restate the history of the neurodiversity movement, as that work has already been done. We highly recommend 'Autistic Community and the Neurodiversity Movement: Stories from the Frontline' (Kapp, 2020) for those who wish to explore that history in depth.

Instead, this book focuses on the lived experiences of neurodivergent scholars navigating the current academic milieu. An environment in which neurodivergence can be simultaneously celebrated and marginalised, where institutions signal inclusivity while implementing policies that disproportionately harm neurodivergent scholars, and where disclosure can feel like either a lifeline or a threat to one's career (Brown & Leigh, 2018; Mellifont, 2023; Sarchet, 2024). To meet this aim, we adopt a broad definition of neurodivergent, following (Rosqvist et al., 2020, p. 1) which includes people with 'perceived variations seen in cognitive, affectual, and sensory functioning differing from the majority of the general population or "predominant neurotype"'.

As neurodivergent people ourselves, we have found collective storytelling to be an effective way to make meaning of our experiences and the systems we move within. This book shares stories from neurodivergent researchers across career stages, each centred on a topic that speaks to their experiences. We wrote this book for neurodivergent academics, to share in our challenges and joys, and in doing so, to feel less alone. We also wrote this book for neurotypical academics who wish to better understand their neurodivergent colleagues and students.

This chapter sets the scene for the chapters that follow. We outline the broader academic conditions shaping neurodivergent working lives, introduce the authors and themes that structure the book and describe several key concepts that recur across chapters, namely the double empathy problem, masking and burnout. While no single person, context or story can capture the full breadth of neurodivergent experiences, we hope these narratives and concepts resonate with readers and help guide their journey through this book and through their careers in the academia.

THE CLIMATE OF ACADEMIA FOR NEURODIVERGENT SCHOLARS

Although we have been in academia for a relatively short period of time, we have noticed increasing demands on academics over this period. Multiple data points suggest that our perceptions are real, including the need for this *Surviving and Thriving in Academia* series of books. A prevalent narrative in educational discourse suggests that academia has been profoundly reshaped by neoliberal reforms, fundamentally altering both the purpose ('why') and methodology ('how') of work within higher education institutions. These changes are characterised by increased marketisation, a heightened emphasis on quantifiable metrics and a shift away from the traditional view of universities as institutions primarily serving the public good (Bosio & Olssen, 2023). Our respective mentors, all of whom have been in academia for decades longer than we have, confirm that times truly are different.

These shifts are gaining recognition worldwide, inside and outside of academia. At the time of writing, the Australian Senate Standing Committees on Education and Employment's (2025) '*Quality of governance at Australian higher education providers*' final report was just released. This report articulated the growing concerns of diverse stakeholders – including students, professional staff, academics and university administrators – that Australian universities have been operating excessively like for-profit corporations, rather than as institutions primarily dedicated to serving the public interest.

Discussions with colleagues around the world suggest that higher education's orientation towards profit at the expense of social mission is a global problem, affecting institutions regardless of age, status or size. These shifts have had a damning impact on academic employment across the career spectrum, including the imposition of onerous administrative burdens on individuals without formal training in workplace law, economics or project management, often through business improvement plans. This stress has been compounded by escalating expectations related to publication metrics and precarious employment conditions that push academics to focus on short-term survival rather than long-term career planning.

There is a growing body of research showing that these burdens are especially challenging for neurodivergent academics. For example, in his narrative literature review Mellifont (2023) explored the interaction between stigma and these modern professional pressures. He highlighted concerns around neurodivergence being disbelieved or being used as an excuse for underperformance, a concern echoed by participants from our own study within our institution (Riordan et al., 2024). Mellifont's reference to Brown and Leigh's (2018) findings regarding attitudes towards invisible disabilities is particularly unsettling. In Brown and Leigh's study, 'hidden disabilities' were perceived as a way for people to either avoid doing the required academic work or as a way to escape scrutiny for their quality of work. When taking into consideration the shaping of higher education systems into 'machines' concerned with outputs and outcomes, neurodivergent people are often seen as pebbles in the gears of neoliberal optimisation.

AUTHORS FROM A RANGE OF BACKGROUNDS TELLING THEIR STORIES

The writing of this book was a collective process. We met repeatedly to discuss our plans, share reflections on our chapters and clarify our core messages. Through this process, it became clear that what we wanted to write together was deeper and more personal than we had initially imagined. While we celebrate the joy of finding communities and spaces that have meaning to us, we have not always been understood and supported in academia. We were intentional about not sugar-coating experiences that have caused (and are causing) pain within our neurodivergent research community. Many of us have felt blindsided by unwritten rules, inflexible management, inhospitable environments and impossible expectations. At the same time, we have also experienced the joy and meaning that come from finding spaces and teams that let us exist as ourselves and work to our strengths.

We hope that being honest about both our positive and negative circumstances will help to prepare and bolster the next generation of neurodivergent researchers, while letting our colleagues who have already experienced (or are experiencing) these challenges know that they are not alone. We also hope that neurotypical academics who read this book may come to understand more deeply what their neurodivergent colleagues may be experiencing. For too long there has been the expectation that neurodivergent people learn to use and understand neurotypical communication – a labour that is not often reciprocated (e.g. Finke & Dunn, 2023).

The chapters that follow are first-person accounts from neurodivergent academics across the career spectrum, each focusing on a theme the author felt impassioned to impart. Katie Munday begins by detailing the process and challenges of deciding to become a researcher, including finding PhD supervisors who respect and understand both their neurodivergent and trans identities, the joys of connecting with other lived-experience researchers, and their wariness of universities as capitalist institutions. Jessica Riordan follows with her account of finishing a PhD and attempting to find employment. She shares how well-meaning advice to have a baby during one's PhD because 'the publication clock doesn't start until you finish' intersected with constant moves, health challenges and undiagnosed ADHD and autism to make both completion and employment feel almost impossible.

Sarah Timperley then reflects on how barriers to doing well are often more to do with people than research skills and that naivety, anxiety and honesty (which can come across as a complete lack of tact) can all contribute to a rocky start to an academic career. Next, Jenny Mai Phan discusses how imposter syndrome can be an inevitable consequence of internalised ableism, neurotypical-centric advice and institutional practices. She draws on her experience as an Asian and autistic[1] woman working in a mostly white neurotypical field to talk about how identity multiplies these barriers.

---

[1]We recognise that some people prefer to capitalise 'Autistic' to indicate that they are using a cultural conceptualise of the neurotype, while others prefer 'autistic'. Throughout this book we have allowed the individual authors to choose their preference for their piece of writing.

As an academic further along in her career, Kathryn E Ringland takes the reader through her experiences of burnout as a constant state. She describes how her own commitment to doing the emotional labour that allows others to survive clashes against a system that makes this work invisible in its constant drive for output, as well as how the community of empathy she has created stands in defiance of these systems. We then hear from Mario Liong, who writes about his navigation of neurodivergence within academic systems in East Asia. He describes the tensions caused by interactions between the external sensory environment and the pressures he has put on himself. He discusses how sensory sensitivity and disability are seen within the cultures he's worked in and how this impacts him as an academic.

Matthew Harrison's chapter focuses on the challenge of creating innovation within entrenched systems, particularly when many people within these systems seem intent on keeping the status quo. He then discusses the balance between placating and pushing and how understanding and having empathy for those who might object has helped him create change without making others feel left behind. In her chapter, Sandra C. Thom-Jones also explores the challenges that success can bring, reflecting on working with teams that respected and supported her ways of being, the type of leadership she offered as an autistic academic and the respect and support she gave to those who worked for her. Sandra also describes her move into a higher leadership role, where the disbanding of her team and unpredictable role changes ultimately led her to leave academia.

Our final chapter brings together nine neurodivergent researchers who are early in their research career and/or work outside of the usual university system. Through short vignettes, they describe their journeys towards finding community and purpose. Their stories show how the next generation of researchers is taking up the mantle and working together with other neurodivergent and disabled scholars and community members to create a world where we can all thrive. Across these diverse accounts, common threads emerge to form patterns that extend beyond individual circumstance and point towards shared experiences that have been shaped by systemic norms.

SHARED CONCEPTS INFORMING THIS BOOK

Although the authors in this book identify with a wide range of intersecting neurotypes and social positions, several concepts recur across chapters. In particular, the double empathy problem, masking and autistic burnout provide a common language for describing the experiences of misunderstanding, adaptation and the concomitant exhaustion that accompanies working within largely neurotypically oriented academic environments. While these concepts originated in efforts to articulate autistic experiences, they have since been adopted by other neurominorities as ways of naming shared patterns of experience across marginalised neurotypes. Ultimately, we believe these concepts help in communicating how difference is negotiated within largely neurotypically structured worlds.

The Double Empathy Problem

The double empathy problem reconceptualises communication challenges as a mutual breakdown in understanding between people with different neurotypes, rather than a deficit located solely within neurominorities (particularly autistic individuals). The concept was articulated by Damian Milton, drawing on social and relational theories of communication to challenge deficit-based models of autism (Milton, 2012). It proposes that difficulties arise because neurotypical norms dominate social expectations, marginalising alternative ways of communicating and being. While not without detractors (for example, see Bollen & van Grunsven, 2025), many neurodivergent people find this lens validating because it reframes lifelong experiences of misunderstanding, exclusion and misinterpretation as relational and systemic, not personal failures, within a predominantly neurotypically-normed world.

Masking and the Associated Risks

Masking refers to the conscious or unconscious suppression of neurodivergent traits to conform to neurotypical social norms. The term emerged from autistic-led scholarship and lived experience accounts describing strategies used to avoid stigma, exclusion or harm. Masking can include mimicking social behaviours, hiding sensory needs or overregulating emotions. While it may enable short-term social access, extensive research links masking to significant detriments, including exhaustion, anxiety, depression, burnout (see the following section), reduced self-concept clarity and delayed identification or support (Chapman et al., 2022; Cleary et al., 2023; Miller et al., 2021). For many neurodivergent people, understanding masking explains chronic stress and identity strain produced by navigating environments that privilege neurotypical ways of being.

Autistic Burnout

Finally, autistic burnout describes a state of pervasive physical, emotional and cognitive exhaustion experienced by autistic people following prolonged stress and unmet support needs. It is commonly associated with sustained masking, sensory overload, social pressure and repeated demands to function within neurotypically structured environments. Burnout is characterised by a loss of skills, reduced tolerance for stimuli, increased shutdowns or meltdowns and diminished capacity for daily tasks (Arnold et al., 2023). Unlike occupational burnout, autistic burnout is thought to reflect a systemic mismatch rather than individual resilience (Higgins et al., 2021). Many autistic people find the concept empowering because it legitimises experiences of collapse and recovery as predictable responses to chronic exclusion, overload and unrealistic expectations.

CONCLUSION

Together, the stories in this book make visible the varied yet connected worlds neurodivergent academics are asked to navigate. These worlds are often shaped by structural pressures, relational misunderstandings and the ongoing emotional and physical labour of surviving (and at times resisting) neurotypically structured academic systems. By collating our stories, we have actively chosen to resist the individualistic and fragmented nature of academia that so often hides harm, asserting instead that what happens to neurodivergent academics is not incidental but structural.

At the same time, we are incredibly aware of the privilege we authors hold as people who have both the space and social capital to share our stories openly. Though these stories were challenging for many of us to share, there are still many neurodivergent academics (and neurodivergent people more broadly) across the world for whom contributing to a work like this would carry real risk: whether through overt punishment, subtle stereotyping or the operation of governmental and institutional policies. Others are simply fighting too many battles on too many fronts to have the capacity to participate in even more. As racism, ableism, transphobia, homophobia, sexism and a host of other forms of violence intensify globally, we recognise that many of our neurodivergent colleagues are pushing for acceptance and change on more fronts than we can see. To all our neurodivergent colleagues across the globe, take care out there.

In closing, we wish to propose care as the necessary companion to resistance. Care for ourselves, one another and for the world, guided by the hope that the world may one day be a more just, humane and liveable place for all of us to thrive.

REFERENCES

Arnold, S. R., Higgins, J. M., Weise, J., Desai, A., Pellicano, E., & Trollor, J. N. (2023). Confirming the nature of autistic burnout. *Autism*, 27(7), 1906–1918. https://doi.org/10.1177/13623613221147410

Australian Senate Standing Committee on Education and Employment, C. (2025). *Quality of governance at Australian higher education providers – Final report* (Australia). [Text]. https://www.aph.gov.au/Parliamentary_Business/Committees/Senate/Education_and_Employment/UniversityGovernance48/Final_report

Bollen, C., & van Grunsven, J. (2025). In defence of the double empathy problem hypothesis: An urgently needed alternative to fallacies and injustices in mainstream autism research. *Psychological Review*. https://doi.org/10.1037/rev0000605

Bosio, E., & Olssen, M. (2023). Critical global citizenship: Foucault as a complexity thinker, social justice and the challenges of higher education in the era of neo-liberal globalization – A conversation with Mark Olssen. *Citizenship Teaching & Learning*, *18*, 245–261. https://doi.org/10.1386/ctl_00123_1

Brown, N., & Leigh, J. (2018). Ableism in academia: Where are the disabled and ill academics?. *Disability & Society*, *33*(6), 985–989. https://doi.org/10.1080/09687599.2018.1455627

Chapman, L., Rose, K., Hull, L., & Mandy, W. (2022). "I want to fit in… but I don't want to change myself fundamentally": A qualitative exploration of the relationship between masking and mental health for autistic teenagers. *Research in Autism Spectrum Disorders*, *99*, 102069. https://doi.org/10.1016/j.rasd.2022.102069

Cleary, M., West, S., Kornhaber, R., & Hungerford, C. (2023). Autism, discrimination and masking: Disrupting a recipe for trauma. *Issues in Mental Health Nursing*, *44*(9), 799–808. https://doi.org/10.1080/01612840.2023.2239916

Finke, E. H., & Dunn, D. H. (2023). Neurodiversity and double empathy: Can empathy disconnects be mitigated to support autistic belonging?. *Disability & Society*, *0*(0), 1–24. https://doi.org/10.1080/09687599.2023.2295802

Higgins, J. M., Arnold, S. R., Weise, J., Pellicano, E., & Trollor, J. N. (2021). Defining autistic burnout through experts by lived experience: Grounded Delphi method investigating #AutisticBurnout. *Autism*, *25*(8), 2356–2369. https://doi.org/10.1177/13623613211019858

S. K., Kapp (Ed.) (2020), *Autistic community and the neurodiversity movement: Stories from the frontline*. Springer. https://doi.org/10.1007/978-981-13-8437-0

Mellifont, D. (2023). *Ableist ivory towers: A narrative review informing about the lived experiences of neurodivergent staff in contemporary higher education*. https://doi.org/10.1080/09687599.2021.1965547

Miller, D., Rees, J., & Pearson, A. (2021). "Masking is life": Experiences of masking in autistic and nonautistic adults. *Autism in Adulthood*, *3*(4), 330–338. https://doi.org/10.1089/aut.2020.0083

Milton, D. E. M. (2012). On the ontological status of autism: The 'double empathy problem'. *Disability & Society*, *27*(6), 883–887. https://doi.org/10.1080/09687599.2012.710008

Riordan, J., Timperley, S., O'Brien, C., Edwards, C., Murrihy, C., Harrison, M., McKay-Brown, L., & Mendus, A. (2024). Creating the conditions for inclusion: Investigating optimal physical spaces for supporting neurodivergent staff and postgraduate students. *Neurodiversity*, *2*, 27546330241285353. https://doi.org/10.1177/27546330241285353

Rosqvist, H. B., Chown, N., & Stenning, A. (Eds). (2020). *Neurodiversity studies: A new critical paradigm* (1st ed.). Routledge. https://doi.org/10.4324/9780429322297

Sarchet, L. N. (2024). Experiences of disabled and neurodivergent faculty in higher education: A systematic literature review. *Journal of Disability Studies in Education*. https://doi.org/10.1163/25888803-bja10032

Tan, D. W., Rabuka, M., Haar, T., & Pellicano, E. (2024). 'It's a symbolic violence': Autistic people's experiences of discrimination at universities in Australia. *Autism*, *28*(6), 1344–1356. https://doi.org/10.1177/13623613231219744

2

BETWEEN RESEARCH AND RESISTANCE: INSIGHTS FROM A TRANS NEURODIVERGENT PHD STUDENT

KATIE MUNDAY

University of Portsmouth, UK

ABSTRACT

This chapter explores the lived experience of undertaking a PhD as a trans, neurodivergent researcher in the United Kingdom. Using personal narrative and autoethnographic reflection, it considers how academic systems shaped by hierarchy, productivity and normative assumptions create barriers to belonging for marginalised students. The chapter situates the doctoral study within the broader context of the COVID-19 pandemic, family life and community activism, highlighting how research is never separate from lived realities. It reflects on the process of building supervisory relationships, navigating epistemic injustice and finding solidarity within queer, disabled and neurodivergent communities. Central to this account is the tension of being both researcher and community member and the exhaustion and joy that come with occupying this dual role.

Keywords: Autistic; trans; epistemic injustice; non-hierarchical; community

Source: Artwork by Abby Lastowski.
A Portrait of Katie Munday.

STARTING OUT

If you told me in my early 20s that I'd do a university degree, I probably would have said, 'What on earth would I do a degree in?!' Throughout my school years, I was led to believe that there were only two choices after school: a manual job or further education. My school funnelled students into one of two pathways: one in which students would take up a trade, and the second was a clear path to college and university. Neither of those restrictive pathways did anything for me, and by the time I had finished college, I was sick of being told I *needed* to attend university. So, I took a nine-year gap year, and in those years, I got to know a lot about myself and what I wanted from life (and what I did *not* want from life). I went from a shop worker and training as a baker to volunteering overseas and coming home to retrain as an early year's educator. I often refer to myself as an accidental academic; it was not a lifelong dream or ambition. It was never on the radar for me to achieve much of anything.

Due to my lengthy gap year, I was considered a 'mature student' in my undergraduate course, where I studied childhood and youth studies with psychology. I liked studying, and unlike my predicted grades for A levels (college grades in the UK), I was pretty good at it! I often felt like the odd one out in many of my classes, although I was yet to fully understand why; even with the other mature students, I just didn't quite fit. This was by no means a new feeling for me, but the realisation of why I felt this came to light in my work outside of the university. At the time, I was working as a youth leader, working with disabled and neurodivergent young people, and when I saw how they engaged with sensory elements of the world, how dedicated many of them were to their interests, and how they spoke with each other, it unlocked something in me.

When I met new young people and their families to do their initial paperwork, I saw myself reflected in them so many times. There were so many occasions where I left the family's home believing I had met a younger version of myself. There was a young person who came to wheelchair basketball who used to zoom around and miaow like a cat – something that I often liked to join in with, albeit slower (but always *louder*). I was not expecting to find belonging and self-understanding with a group of five to 12-year-olds, but that's the beauty of youth work. I sat with this realisation for a long time before I spoke to my doctor and got my formal diagnosis in the final year of my undergraduate studies. To the credit of the university, I was given a lot of support in that final year, including long-term wellbeing support and additional time with exams, all while I wrote my dissertation on how to support LGBTQIA + autistic students![1]

In the same year that I was diagnosed as autistic and with OCD, not long after I graduated from my undergraduate studies, COVID-19 broke out. Everyone in the United Kingdom, and across the world, was left to make choices about their health with

---

[1]I shared some of my findings here: https://autisticltd.co.uk/2025/12/03/supporting-trans-autistic-young-people-in-schools/

no knowledge, resources or support. My undergraduate graduation was moved online, and I didn't go, I couldn't face this last-minute change and to 'go' to my graduation when the world was falling apart. Despite feeling like the world was going to collapse at any moment, the natural progression onto a master's course was just that: natural. I finally understood that I enjoyed learning, and I was keen to explore a similar area to my undergraduate thesis. I undertook a master's in research, which was hands-on and self-led. I interviewed 12 trans and gender-diverse (TGD) autistic adults about their life experiences, including mental health, relationships, aspirations, employment and recommendations for future research on TGD autistic experiences (Munday, 2024; Munday et al., 2025). I had hoped to interview people in person, but that was made impossible by COVID-19 restrictions, which had also furloughed me from work.

Two months into my master's in research (MRes) – when it was clear that the COVID-19 restrictions were going to become long-term – I found out that I was pregnant. I immediately changed my studies from full-time on-campus to part-time off-campus. I continued to study at home in the bubble[2] of my husband and mum. Living with my immunocompromised husband and worrying about my brother, who had a kidney transplant the previous year, tensions were very high, so I poured myself into my work. I said 'yes' to every opportunity that came my way, to keep myself from despairing at home, pregnant and scared. One of these opportunities was to mentor another master's student who studied the accessibility of gender identity healthcare for autistic people. We later published this work before she welcomed her own bundle of joy into the world (Bruce et al., 2023), and that is how I met Steven Kapp, my eventual PhD supervisor and friend (more on him later).

I finished my MRes in 2022 and then took a well-needed gap year (just the one this time!). I wasn't sure I wanted to do a PhD, as it felt like every time I walked into the academy, I had a massive

[2]'Bubble' was the term for a small group of people that you could safely interact with during the COVID-19 lockdowns in the United Kingdom. You were only able to talk to and be with these people throughout the lockdown periods.

personal realisation, or an outbreak of a deadly virus happened. Studies were never plain sailing, of course, but at this point, I felt it was taking the piss. With all that had happened personally and globally over those years, I did the only thing I could: I slowly returned to work, running a youth group. Returning to work is one thing, but returning from a state-mandated lockdown with a baby was something else. The group I worked with was physically and socially vulnerable to the virus and the social restrictions. It was an unsettling time for them, going back to school and the so called 'normal'. And it was an unsettling time for me to go back into the world as a new mom, chronically ill and working with vulnerable young people. Until I wrote this chapter, I hadn't realised how much COVID-19 and the restrictions had affected me. I had kept my head down through it all and clung tightly to the structure and purpose that research afforded me. It was a truly terrifying time, and I understand that COVID-19 still bars many immuno-compromised people from living the lives they want. I'm so thankful that my family and I remained safe, and I often think about those who didn't make it.

FINDING MY SUPERVISORS

Deciding to do a PhD was the first step in a long process. I needed to work out what I wanted to focus on, and then came the difficult task of organising my supervisory team. Was I going to stay at the University of Portsmouth? Was I going to move further afield? Who would be both gender *and* neuro-affirming? How was I going to pay for this? And how would all this work around our little family? All these questions I had to consider before I applied.

There was a lot of administration that came with finding a supervisory team. Going for the South Coast Doctoral Training Partnership[3] (SCDTP) funding meant that I had four universities to choose from. I looked through the four hard-to-navigate university

---

[3]South Coast Doctoral Training Partnership, funded by the Economic and Social Research Council, awards 34 studentships per year across four universities on the south coast of the United Kingdom https://southcoastdtp.ac.uk/

websites to find potential supervisors, and there were different levels of interest and engagement from those I emailed. I quickly learned to create a template which I tailored to each potential supervisor, which worked well apart from the one time I forgot to change someone's name (I am still recovering from this social blunder!). Administration is not my favourite thing. Being autistic (and likely ADHD) adds an additional interesting dimension to this menial task. SCDTP funding is highly sought after, and there was no guarantee I would be awarded. All this effort could have been for naught; there was simply no way that I could work full-time while doing a PhD and parenting a young child (fair play to those who can and do).

Finding a supervisor was a mixed experience for me; I needed to feel safe and supported with my neurocognitive style and my gender queerness. When looking for a supervisor, I consulted several sociology lecturers, one of whom warned me against moving to psychology from sociology. They suggested that my approach would not fit well within a psychology department. As I have shared previously (Munday, 2025b), I am yet to burst into flames from crossing the school threshold. Whichever school I ended up in, it was important for me to have lived experience supervisors; I could find autistic academics, and trans and/or queer ones, but none of the queer autistic academics had the capacity to supervise another PhD student. The one person I knew I wanted as a supervisor was Steven. I had enjoyed my time working with him alongside one of his master's students, and I had admired his work for many years. He exemplifies for me how autistic-led research negotiates the thin, winding, blurry line between research and activism, what Botha (2021) has described as a 'delicate line between "personal" and "professional"' (p.1).

I knew Steven would respect my work and my trans and Disabled identities. My second and third supervisors were similarly straightforward choices; I was working with Chris Papadopoulos at the Autistic Substance Use Network (see some of our work here: Munday et al., 2025; Papadopoulos et al., 2025), and Emine Gurbuz, who has lots of experience in leading participatory research with autistic adults. Unfortunately, Chris took a step back from academia and could no longer be my third supervisor, but he continues to be a source of support. There was a short-lived moment of panic before Mel Hughes, whom I had worked with previously on cancer service research (Tansley et al., 2024, NIHR, 2025), took the third supervisor position. Even with this change, I appreciate that creating a supervisory team is often much more complex and that some students do not get to choose their team.

I want to share a story about Steven (with his permission, of course). The story starts on a windy day at the seafront, the kind of weather that is both too hot for a coat and also raining. I had signed up to hold a giant trans pride flag leading the parade at Portsmouth Pride.[4] I shared this honour with 100 community members and allies, including Steven. Halfway through the walk, I got a little tearful. I spoke to the person in front of me while pointing at Steven, who was wearing a raincoat and holding the opposite side of the flag. I said: 'You don't know me, but I just want to let you know that that man there is my PhD supervisor. He's not trans, but he wanted to come today to support me. I got him the Choose Love hat that he's wearing'. Steven's flag-bearing was a well-timed reminder that there are people who care about and show up for trans people and that sometimes these people show up in the most unexpected of places.

FINDING MY COMMUNITY

At the time of writing, I have been a PhD student for a year. The last year has been a flurry of activity, confusion, and connecting (and sometimes clashing) with others. One thing that has remained constant is my coming out in the first few sentences of meeting other researchers. This includes the first PowerPoint slide with 'they/he' written on it. My walking stick, my 'outside' voice, stimming and fidget toys, and my occasional sitting or lying on the floor. I cannot, and will not, remain closeted as a trans, queer, mad, disabled person. This leaves me open to prejudice, and I expend far too much energy in identifying and navigating unsafe situations. Coming out as trans in academic spaces is a sure-fire

[4]Portsmouth Pride https://www.portsmouthpride.org.uk/

way to detect closed-minded people, but it also allows me to connect with others who centre their research and lives around social justice.

In early 2025, I was lucky enough to spend some time with other queer researchers and allies at the Queer Methodologies in Medical Humanities PhD School at Durham University.[5] I was thrilled to meet Monique Botha and Amy Pearson for a cup of coffee before the event. I had worked previously with Monique on the Boycott Spectrum 10K[6] campaign but had never met them in person, and I've been a long-time admirer of Amy's work. I was meant to meet them at the centre where the PhD school was, but we didn't know that the centre would be closed, have no coffee facilities and be at the top of a staircase known locally as 'Mount Olympus'. This is when I decided it might be nice for them to pick me up and drive us all to the botanical gardens (which were also shut). We eventually landed at the café near their university building. A classically disorganised neurodivergent outing. It was such a joy to spend time with them both and talk about autism research and moan collectively about various things.

The PhD school itself facilitated an amazing group of queer researchers and methodology scholars. We had so much fun and laughed so much during our three days together. Eating at food courts, drinking wine and lying on the floor watching Preciado's Orlando: My Political Biography (2023). We went shopping together in a local Tesco Express – a first time for some of the Indian students, which I believe is well-documented in some of their diaries! We ate together, looked after each other, checked in, made zines and drank a lot of terrible coffee. The image of Landa Mabenge[7] dragging himself back from a trip to a local restaurant, screaming, 'Why has Durham got so many fucking hills?' while

---

[5]The Queer Methodologies in Medical Humanities PhD School was a Wellcome Trust-funded event at Durham University, United Kingdom, in early 2025 https://medhumsplatform.org/queer-methodologies-in-medical-humanities-reflections-on-our-phd-school

[6]Boycott Spectrum 10K was a successful campaign to stop the DNA collection of 10,000 autistic people in the United Kingdom by the Autism Research Centre of Cambridge University https://aucademy.co.uk/2021/09/03/boycott-spectrum-10k-please-sign/

[7]Landa Mabenge, author and consultant https://landamconsulting.co.za/

laughing his head off, will remain firmly in my memories. I have kept in contact with many of the Queer Methodologies attendees and went to London Trans + Pride 2025 with one of the group members who was visiting the United Kingdom that summer.

More locally, I have begun to connect with other like-minded (often neurodivergent) PhD students and researchers. I am part of a non-binary research group, which brings me an enormous amount of joy. I have also had the pleasure of running a hybrid symposium with two other PhD students, talking on the intersections of sociology with crip theory, critical disability studies and mad studies.[8] I am lucky to call many of these people my friends. I am glad to have made connections with others that show me that my 'radical' research ideas are sometimes shared. I am delighted to be around amazing scholars who strive to dismantle, disrupt, and challenge formal ways of knowing. Who challenges the notion of what and who 'counts' in knowledge creation?

FINDING (AND KEEPING) MYSELF

Despite connections with other neurodivergent researchers, there is an undercurrent of unspoken but enacted and embodied politics throughout my school and university. I knew there was going to be more politics as I got further into the academy, but I was not ready for the intensity of it. Aside from the typical tensions of labouring under capitalism, I have witnessed and experienced some horrific behaviour. Some academics are too entrenched in hierarchy, position and power dynamics to treat people, especially students and others deemed 'underneath' them, as human beings. Some are so worried about their career prospects and financial security that they will clamber over whoever and whatever (including their own principles, if they ever had any) to reach the top. I will not centre these behaviours or the people responsible for them; however, it would be remiss of me to ignore the violence faced by marginalised researchers within the academy.

[8]The Intersections of Sociology with Crip Theory, Critical Disability Studies and Mad Studies Symposium, 2025. https://autisticltd.co.uk/2025/06/20/exploring-crip-theory-insights-from-our-hybrid-symposium/

I came to academia in a sideways manner – first, I was an activist, then a researcher, and now I am an accidental academic. The academy did not call me. I remain uncharmed by its empty promises of excellence, expertise and superiority. I stay unenamoured with the notions of centring control and hierarchy. Universities sell a product; they want bums on seats, and they'll use league tables, hollow certifications and awards, and much more to draw potential students in. What these universities are not selling (because they have not bought into it themselves) is the joy of creating knowledge and the importance of sharing this freely with all. They are not selling community, connection, and liberation; they are selling capitalism on performance-enhancing drugs. Finding myself in the academy physically, spiritually, and psychologically continues to be difficult.

I constantly ask myself whether doing trans-and gender-diverse autistic research within the academy is the right move. There remains a tragic irony in doing my research in a system that continues to harm my community. I continue to reflect on my intention, and I am ready to take accountability for any harm that I commit. I grapple with these feelings constantly. This is largely why I continue to coach wheelchair basketball and organise with local disability and trans groups. I am figuring out how to do work that bridges activism and academia because my research is not theoretical to me. I am not a researcher or a community member; I am both. I reside in the liminal space of research, activism, and lived experience. And it's exhausting.

This exhaustion follows me into academic writing – I am often stuck between what I really want (and need) to say and what I *should* say. I *should* be more professional, use indecipherable nomenclature and talk about my community as if I were not a part of it. I find writing with other neurodivergent people much more freeing; there is so much I do not have to explain about my autisticness, my queerness, my me-ness. There is also an underlying current of flat hierarchy in these collaborations – knowledge and insight are appreciated from all spheres of formal, informal, and non-existent education. There's something very real about that. I've been given some amazing opportunities to write about shifting research paradigms in gender-diverse autistic research, and the double empathy problem applied to trans autistic experiences in healthcare (Munday, 2024a and Munday, 2025a, respectively). I've even been able to reflect on the inaccessibility of ethics applications in universities (Munday, 2024b). I am honoured to write among some truly great neurodivergent thinkers; I am just waiting to accept myself as one too.

A PROMISE

With my haphazard journey and brain in mind, I wanted to end my chapter with a promise: I promise to consistently insist on taking up space in academia as a trans autistic person. I promise that I will not dim my power and that I will remain unapologetic about who I am and how I engage with academia. This includes my fumbled networking, chronic pain, brain fog, swearing in meetings, swearing *at* supervisors, emails filed in the bin, 100 cups of coffee and 100 open tabs. I promise I will remain ambivalent to the hierarchies within my institution. I will not value titles, but I *will* observe how the responsibilities (and power) given to the titled are wielded or neglected. I promise to continue falling in love with knowledge in all the ways it is created, learned, shared, explored and articulated. I promise to stay true to myself, to honour myself, and to know when it is time to say 'enough'.

REFERENCES

Botha, M. (2021). Academic, activist, or advocate? Angry, entangled, and emerging: A critical reflection on autism knowledge production. *Frontiers in Psychology*, *12*, 1–12. https://doi.org/10.3389/fpsyg.2021.727542

Bruce, H., Munday, K., & Kapp, S. K. (2023). Exploring the experiences of autistic transgender and non-binary adults in seeking gender identity healthcare. *Autism and Adulthood*, *5*(2), 191–203. https://doi.org/10.1089/aut.2023.0003

Munday, K. (2024a). Shifting research paradigms in gender diverse autistic research. In H. Bertilsdotter-Rosqvist, A. Day, & M. Krazinski's (Eds.), *Living under a double rainbow: Exploring autistic genders, sexualities, and relationality* (pp. 46–58). Routledge.

Munday, K. (2024b). The inaccessibility of UK universities ethics applications in humanities and social sciences. In H. Bertilsdotter-Rosqvist & D. Jackson-Perry's (Eds.), *Neurodiversity studies: Research ethics and methods* (pp. 309–324). Palgrave.

Munday, K. (2025a). Double empathy and the double rainbow: Healthcare inequities for gender diverse Autistic adults. In D. Milton's (Ed.), *Double empathy reader* (pp. 433–442). Pavilion.

Munday, K. (2025b, July 29). Radical joy: Rethinking research in health and social care. *Polyphony*. https://thepolyphony.org/2025/07/29/radical-joy-rethinking-research-in-health-and-social-care/

Munday, K., Papadopoulos, C., Adkin, T., & Gray-Hammond, D. (2025). Improving substance use services for autistic adults: Insights and recommendations from autistic adults. *Autism in Adulthood*, *00*(00), 1–13.

Papadopoulos, C., Adkin, T., Munday, K., & Gray-Hammond, D. (2025). Predictors of depression and anxiety among self-medicating autistic adults. *Neurodiversity*, *3*. https://doi.org/10.1177/27546330251344453

Preciado, P. B. (Director). (2023). *Orlando, my political biography* [Film]. Les Films du Poisson; The Criterion Collection.

Research, National Institute for Health and Care. (2025). Whatever it takes. *NIHR Open Research*, *5*(72), 72. https://doi.org/10.3310/nihropenres.1115259.1

Tansley, R., Corbin-Clarke, S., Munday, K., Durrant, A., & Hughes, M. (2024). "What I would like to say" findings: Cancer care for everyone. *Journal of Community Nursing*, *38*(1), 46–50. https://www.jcn.co.uk/journals/issue/02-2024/article/what-i-would-like-to-say-findings-cancer-care-for-everyone

3

NAVIGATING UNEXPECTED DETOURS DURING THE TRANSITION FROM STUDENT TO ACADEMIC CAREER

JESSICA RIORDAN

The University of Melbourne, Australia

ABSTRACT

The journey from PhD to employment is rarely smooth, as informal networks, hidden curricula and hiring freezes can make the academic job market seem inaccessible. To highlight some of the challenges for neurodivergent people, Dr. Riordan frames this transition as a 'Great New Zealand Road Trip'; charting the journey of an undiagnosed neurodivergent woman navigating unexpected detours, breakdowns, rest stops and repeated recalculations. Drawing on lived experience, Jessica discusses how pregnancy, early parenthood, geographic mobility, burnout and precarious employment intersected with her neurodivergence to disrupt traditional academic timelines. She also explores how well-intentioned academic advice, particularly for women, can inadvertently compound these challenges. Finally, Jessica shifts the tone. As described in this chapter, her late diagnosis reframed decades of struggle as predictable outcomes of systems misaligned with neurodivergent bodies and minds. With this insight, what began as a tentative return to academia through a short-term job share became the catalyst for collective action. Overall, this chapter challenges deficit-based narratives of 'falling behind' and instead argues for reimagining academic pathways. It encourages neurodivergent scholars to build new roads rather than driving on ones never constructed for them.

Keywords: Neurodivergent women; women in academia; career disruptions; burnout; mothers in academia; academic inequities

Source: Artwork by Melissa Vallence.

A Portrait of Jessica Riordan.

INTRODUCTION

Like many overachieving students, I thought I had my life planned out. The one I was subtly, and not so subtly, trained to expect as the consummate overachiever. A neatly signposted road trip from PhD to an academic job. No breaks, detours or scenic lookouts, and definitely no mechanical breakdowns. My actual path, however, was not smooth. Instead, as an undiagnosed (at the time) neurodivergent woman, it was more of a 'take a wrong turn, get lured by side quests, change vehicles, fall through a wormhole, and somehow still end up roughly where I meant to go' sort of thing. So, although this chapter was only supposed to be about the challenges of finding an academic job, I decided to take you on a journey. The 'Great New Zealand Road Trip,' if you will, which began well before my PhD graduation.

TAKING THE SCENIC ROUTE

Like many neurodivergent academics, my PhD became a series of academic and personal side quests. Some intentional, others less so, but many arose because I was far more energised by the process of research and research translation than by my specific topic – early child language development. With an interest-based nervous system, a strong need for purpose-driven work, and difficulties saying no, I quickly became my department's 'go-to' person. While this role built valuable, transferable skills, it also significantly extended my PhD timeline. Unfortunately, that timeline was also disrupted by bullying from other PhD students – an experience that triggered intense anxiety every time I opened my laptop (and one that would require another chapter to fully unpack).

As real life rarely respects carefully plotted Gantt charts, PhDs also often unfold alongside major adult transitions. During this period, I met and married my husband, who was also completing a PhD in my department. Knowing I wanted children, I was also advised by multiple mentors to get pregnant before submitting my thesis, as the publication clock does not start until after completion. To help me decide, they shared stories of presenting at conferences mere weeks postpartum and passing babies between offices. So, pregnancy also became my plan.

Additionally, since there is an expectation that we should move for the perfect academic job, and there are only eight universities in New Zealand, moving countries became part of our plan. Because positions are competitive, my husband and I also agreed that whoever received the first amazing opportunity would take it and the other would follow. During his PhD, my husband was awarded a Fulbright Scholarship to complete a fellowship at Brown University. So, after completing a mountain of paperwork, we moved to Providence, Rhode Island, with the intention that I would finish my PhD remotely while still trying for a baby.

Now, spoiler alert, as an undiagnosed Autistic ADHDer, this amended plan went comically wrong. Instead of more dopamine-heavy side quests, what I really needed was fewer distractions and a more regulated nervous system so I could work with my monotropic brain. I also found the transition to living in the United States difficult, as transitions can be hard in general for autistic people, but, to add more degrees of difficulty, I found their social rules and structures wildly different from what I knew. Like many neurodivergent women, I was also blessed with a medically complicated pregnancy (Hampton et al., 2022; Sundelin et al., 2018), including hyperemesis that left me bed-bound for months. So, instead of writing from home, I was crawling to the bathroom and sleeping in the bath because I lacked the energy to crawl back. Finally, by the time I was physically well enough to work again, the accumulated stress, isolation and unresolved wounds had finally culminated in autistic burnout. My executive function refused to kick into gear, and, feeling great shame, I requested the maximum amount of official leave that one could take off from a PhD.

PULLING INTO A REST STOP

At the time, however, embracing my decision to focus on motherhood felt like seeing that longed-for break after hours of driving at high speeds. After nothing but the hum of tyres and constant movement, I finally saw it – the arrow pointing towards a rest area. An invitation to pause and enjoy the scenery – not just catch glimpses of other peoples' lives in my periphery. I dreamt of starting my days slowly, full of baby giggles, walks in the sun and time in cafes with other parents. To let love and instinct guide the day, unburdened by the rush and rules of academia. So, with a strange mix of relief and disorientation, I pulled off the academic highway.

As I entered this metaphorical rest area, I knew I had made the right decision. My shoulders dropped, the 'road noise' dulled and I felt a sense of quiet satisfaction. After years of pushing myself to my limit, however, exhaustion finally arrived in my body. Additionally, though my journey had slowed, I still felt in motion. Scanning for hazards that no longer existed. Any mention of my thesis or time spent on my laptop brought the dread rushing back. My heart would pound and shame would seep in. It was excruciating. Embarrassing. I was a failure. I couldn't do it.

So, I ran. Both metaphorically and physically. I would slam my laptop shut and soothe my anxiety by losing myself in baby shops, learning to knit, baking traditional New Zealand goods and crafting for events with friends from Brown University (You should see the paper mâché dragon head I made for our Halloween party!). I also became adept at changing the subject whenever my thesis came up. Everyone loves talking about babies after all, and people wanted to know whether we noticed any differences in healthcare. The answer was yes, by the way. So much so that, after receiving clearance from my obstetrician, I squeezed on the strongest compression stockings I could find and boarded a flight to New Zealand, alone, 35 weeks pregnant (not 35 months, thank you, Air New Zealand flight attendant!). My husband followed a few weeks later.

Interestingly, although maybe not surprising to other autistic academics reading this, this shift in scenery back to the routine and familiarity of my parents' house allowed me to start writing again. My map had finally reoriented itself, and the 'Great Academic Road Trip' was back on. In true autistic pregnancy fashion, however, I barely made it down the road before my body decided to intervene. Again. Although this time it was my liver trying to take me out, and I was under strict orders to rest. I was weirdly okay with this medically induced pause, however, because my spirits were lifted with that brief spark of momentum. I could see it. We were about to meet our daughter, and I would be back on the road in no time.

Once our daughter finally made her dramatic entrance into the world via an emergency c-section (because, of course, she did; transitions are hard, remember!), and my husband submitted his own PhD thesis from the birthing suite(!), my days looked vastly different from the idealised life I had imagined. Yes, there were baby giggles, walks in the sun and pure and utter joy as I watched my baby discover the world, but there were also incessant, loud 'requests' for constant stimulation. Neurodivergent people tend to have neurodivergent babies after all, and our daughter never lasted long doing any one thing. Her protests would get louder and louder until we carried her everywhere, facing forward. Her eyes and grin wide with every new thing she saw.

Like many neurodivergent babies, our daughter also struggled with sleep and feeding (Grant et al., 2022; Spanò et al., 2024). Right from birth, she could, and would, stay awake for unusually long periods. Her naps were also only 20 minutes long and she only slept in 40-minute chunks at night, only settling when held upright and rhythmically soothed. She also struggled to gain weight and we started to suspect she had allergies. We. Were. Tired. So much for my dreams of luxuriating during long naps with cups of hot tea, chipping away at my thesis. Instead, my 'spare time to write' was consumed by weekly weigh-ins and hearing variations of, 'You are just an anxious first-time mum and she can sense it. You need to stop letting her manipulate you, take a sleeping pill, and just let her cry-it-out'. Yeah... since babies literally lack the cognitive ability to manipulate people (Evans & Lee, 2013) and infant sleep has become a special interest of mine, my husband and I refused their advice. Though the fatigue was killing us, we were determined to be her advocates. This tenacity paid off too, as shortly after our daughter turned one, a different paediatrician finally advised us to remove dairy, soy and egg from both our diets. After only three days, our baby started sleeping in three-to-four-hour chunks at nighttime. The damage was done, however. She had now developed feeding aversions and still doesn't eat much seven years later.

Looking back, you can see how the well-intentioned advice to have a baby during my PhD accidentally set me up for a rockier road. Especially when we didn't know I was neurodivergent. Because, for many neurodivergent people, pregnancy isn't a strategic pause but a sensory and medical rollercoaster. Additionally, early parenthood is routine-shattering chaos for everyone and is often extra chaos for those of us with children with support needs. Add in monotropic focus and parenthood becoming a special interest, and the transition back to the workforce becomes nearly impossible. In this instance, what was framed as clever career planning for PhD students can, without meaning to, cause neurodivergent academics to fall even further behind their peers.

SETTING UP CAMP

Like the year before our daughter's birth, we spent the next year and a half constantly moving. Six weeks postpartum, when my muscles and nerves were still trying to knit themselves together, we made the decision to move back to Dunedin so my husband could do some casual work for our old university. Then, three months later, we moved to Sydney, Australia, for his first post-doc. Finally, after six months in our first rental apartment, our apartment was sold, and we had to move. Again. So, between our daughter's sleep and feeding difficulties, I spent this time of my life boxing, unboxing and boxing up my life again. Not the quiet life of babyccinos, playdates and nursery rhymes at the library for which I was so desperately craving. Those boxes haunted my dreams.

Don't get me wrong; I still really enjoyed this period of motherhood and spent a lot of time setting up wonderful experiences for both our daughter and me. We had an absolute blast! The constant novelty of moving and adventure also kept my ADHD well fed with dopamine, which was great for getting stuff done. But I always felt like I was living on the edge of belonging. Motherhood, our daughter's health battles and constant moving had shrunk my world until it was just her, my husband and myself. I had no time, space or mental capacity to think about my thesis or look for jobs at all.

That's the thing, isn't it? When you get to them, rest areas often look vastly different from the pictures splashed over travel blogs. Instead of natural springs and wildflowers, sometimes you get narrow gravel plots. Visas and scholarships expire, funding conditions tighten, supervision contracts have end dates and scientific theories continue to advance. So, like me, many neurodivergent academics try to finish their PhD part-time. For some, this option is framed as a compassionate accommodation. A way to recover from burnout, manage chronic health issues, balance caregiving responsibilities or just survive financially when scholarships run out. For others, however, it often feels like the only option if we ever want to graduate. So, instead of stopping and getting the rest we need, we slow. We limp. We convince ourselves that working in short bursts is sustainable and not still damaging to our health.

Don't get me wrong, there can be real benefits to going part time. You stay connected to your project, maintain a sense of continuity and avoid the administrative and emotional cost of dropping out. But beyond the months added to our candidacy, there are other invisible costs. For example, neurodivergent people are disproportionately impacted by burnout and chronic and fluctuating health issues (Weir et al., 2021), and after years of masking, overachieving and being rewarded for pushing through pain, we often struggle to know our limits. So, by the time we slow down and admit we need support, we are already depleted and make our final pushes through physical and emotional debt. Without external support or access to scholarships, which often require students to study full-time, our 'spare time for rest and recovery' then gets eaten up by employment. Finally, and crucially for this chapter, while we are crawling down the road just trying to survive, the job market doesn't slow down. Opportunities appear and disappear, short-term contracts are filled, networks shift and hiring windows close. As a result, our days often pass with our engines screaming and fuel lights flashing, unsure how long we can keep going like this and wondering whether we will be able to merge back into traffic at all. Not because we lack talent or ambition, but because the road was never constructed for bodies and brains like ours.

EASING THE KEY BACK IN THE IGNITION

Even though I didn't work on my thesis in the first year of our daughter's life, I felt as though I was still living it. Not the deadlines or the academic pressure, but the actual topic. For years, I felt detached from my topic of child language development. I was instead transfixed by the translation of my research. Without consciously trying, I carried all of my learning into our home. I enriched our daughter's world with language until, suddenly, the theory came alive. Long before she could formally speak, she communicated using looks, gestures and sounds. When she surprised us with her first words at seven months, things shifted even more. She had fewer meltdowns because she could now communicate what she wanted – and what she most certainly did NOT want! The part of my research that once felt dry had finally come alive, and I was finally ready to finish writing my PhD. Or, to go back to my analogy of the great New Zealand (or should it now be Australian?) road trip, I was ready to get back on the road.

But, you know what? You know that thing you can't start, keep putting off and feels as daunting as climbing Mount Everest? Even though people swear it is fine and won't take you long? Yeah, sometimes they are right. After signing our daughter up for daycare and some firm nudging from the university, I ended up completing my thesis in just three months. It was even placed on the University of Otago's 'Exceptional Thesis' list (Thank-you interest-based nervous system!) This was fortunate timing, as I hit submit on the fifth of March 2020. Six days before the World Health Organization declared COVID-19 to be a pandemic and seven days before we pulled our daughter out of daycare to start isolating in our one-bedroom apartment. I was back living the stay-at-home mum life. Literally.

So, just as I was preparing to merge back onto the highway of academic life, the open road I'd imagined collapsed into a maze of border closures, detours and towns with no vacancies. Positions dried up, hiring froze and most academic roles advertised during lockdown were either far outside my field or difficult to take on with a young family. The few research positions that somewhat aligned with my expertise were also, quite appropriately, absorbed by people already within those teams. I couldn't even secure a research assistant role to get my foot in the door, as I was repeatedly told that I was overqualified and therefore unaffordable.

I expected these roadblocks, of course. Academic jobs have always been partly about informal networks, hallway conversations and quiet recommendations. What I hadn't anticipated, however, was losing the chance to find an 'in' altogether. Roles once offered to me no longer existed, conferences and casual meet-and-greets vanished overnight and my overseas supervisors had few collaborators where I was locked down. In a system where relationships matter as much as expertise, trying to break into the local academic community from the isolation of my home felt almost impossible. This was especially difficult as a neurodivergent person navigating unspoken social rules and implicit cues, such as when (?!) to insert yourself into a conversation.

It was also hard to know what I could even apply for. The hiring process is riddled with a hidden curriculum that was unknown to me at the time: unwritten rules about 'stretch' roles, how strictly criteria should be interpreted and how much one is expected to soften or embellish their experience – expectations that sit uneasily with my, and many other autistic people's commitment to honesty and literal interpretation. So, instead of moving forward with renewed momentum, I found myself idling again. Map in hand, unsure where to turn.

It is important to state here, however, that despite how difficult this period was, I was also deeply privileged. During this time, my husband secured a strong position in Melbourne, Australia (yes, another move), allowing us to squeeze by financially. He also remained my fiercest advocate, steadfast in his refusal of any talk of applying for jobs outside of my expertise. Even before we knew I was neurodivergent, he understood that work without meaning would drain me completely. So, I waited. I also widened my scope. I explored not-for-profits and start-ups, and even posted an 'about me' on social media.

It was actually this last approach that worked first, as I met an entrepreneur who was developing resources to support children's language development and wanted the support of someone with expertise in this area. Long story short, I ended up turning down that role. There were a few reasons for this refusal, but it was mainly due to the Intellectual Property Agreement. It required me to turn over all work developed in my spare time and surrender future work in this field for a number of years, including working at a university. At the time, I didn't know such clauses rarely hold up. All I knew was that I couldn't in good faith sign it and their lawyers refused to change it. So, I walked away and decided to pivot instead. If I couldn't find a job I loved, perhaps it was time for another kind of beginning. Why not have another baby?

LEARNING ABOUT THE CAR I WAS DRIVING

And what a pivot it was! I don't know why I thought a second pregnancy would be easier than the first. Hope? Denial? The rose-coloured glasses that arrive once your first child reaches a certain age? All we knew was that our family felt unfinished and this felt like the right time to try. Well, hyperemesis returned, my body faltered and, after an even rougher emergency c-section, our youngest daughter arrived. Funnily enough, in the same hospital where my eldest was born. Yes, thanks to another round of lockdowns stranding us in Christchurch during my PhD graduation, we were living with family once more. Hello beautiful chaos – the moment where my neurodivergence finally made itself impossible to ignore.

I am not alone in discovering my neurodivergence later than I should have. Neurodivergence is frequently missed or misdiagnosed in young girls and people assigned female at birth

(Maciver et al., 2025), particularly for those who excel academically, collect awards and/or go on to have successful careers. Our wheels tend to fall off at different points from the 'norm': during postgraduate study, in the transition from the structured world of education to the unpredictability of the academic job market, or – very commonly – when we become parents. After all, parenting introduces a level of cognitive, sensory and emotional load that can't be optimised or outworked. Sleep deprivation, constant interruption and the demand to always be 'on' fracture routines and familiar coping mechanisms like hyperfocus, last-minute sprints and rigid self-control. So, our resilience frays, our houses become buried in clutter and overwhelm grows, causing many of us to internalise our struggles and become relentlessly self-critical – viewing our exhaustion as incompetence and moral failure.

Fortunately, however, I had years of practice under my belt berating myself with that sort of negative self-talk and I knew it wasn't a safe road for me. Especially with two young girls watching my every move. In the sleepless nights of early parenting, I also began to recognise my own life online. What was interesting, however, was that these stories were all tagged 'ADHD', 'autism', and 'neurodivergent'. Now, trust me, the irony is not lost on me that I have a PhD in developmental psychology and did not consider this earlier. Girls and women simply weren't centred in those conversations. But, after doing a deep dive into the literature and immersing myself in conversations online, I gathered the courage to explore whether my lifetime of anxiety was at least partly caused by ADHD.

BUILDING MY OWN ROADS

When it was confirmed that yes, I was indeed an ADHDer, everything snapped into focus. To stick with my road trip analogy, I had finally learned that I was driving a different kind of car – one that operated differently from others and needed completely different fuel. Suddenly, my personal challenges were no longer seen as failures. Instead, they were reframed as predictable outcomes of a nervous system that had been operating in survival mode for too long. And I. Was. Angry. So angry that people were living like I was, failed by the systems that are supposed to identify and support us. So angry that I would read everything I could get my hands on and infodump about this topic to my friends and family, at length.

Now, funnily enough, it was this hyperfixation of mine that eventually got me a job. I was discussing the sorry state of ADHD research with a friend of mine, Dr. Sarah Timperley, who also did her PhD in the same lab as me (albeit after me and not on the same project) and was diagnosed during that time, and she mentioned that she was recently hired by Dr. Matthew Harrison to investigate the lived experience of neurodivergent postgraduate students and academics in one of the faculties at the University of Melbourne (Riordan et al., 2024). Knowing what I had been through, she suggested we job-share and that I ease back into academia through this short-term, flexible position. One that finally fit life with a neurodivergent four-year-old and a six-month-old. She said she could tell how much I missed academia and that it was time to 'come home.'

As it turned out, this short-term job share became the spark for something far larger. As we listened to neurodivergent participants share their experiences, I began to relax, unmask and quickly recognised the need to investigate autism for myself. We also received further confirmation that our own experiences were not outliers. Stories of the same patterns playing out in academic's lives were shared with us time and again, activating our neurodivergent justice sensitivity. Together with Matt, we were adamant that it was unethical to simply publish these stories and move on. We needed to understand how widespread these experiences were across our university and act with scale, visibility and urgency. First though, we had to convince someone to hire us so we could begin.

Rather than navigating layers of committees and red tape often seen within academia (see chapters from Kate Ringland and Matthew Harrison), we took a different approach – including sending an ambitious email to the Vice-Chancellor at the time, Professor Duncan Maskell. We shared a short video outlining our pilot findings, how they connected to broader institutional challenges and our vision for change. To our surprise and immense relief, our VC caught our vision. With support from the then Dean of Education, Professor Jim Watterston, the Vice-Chancellor committed two years of funding to launch the University of Melbourne Neurodiversity Project – an interdisciplinary initiative focused on better supporting neurodivergent staff and students at the University of Melbourne.

After years of detours and dead ends, driving by instinct, pulling over when exhausted and recalculating after every unexpected turn in the road, this was it. I could finally see a stretch of open road that made sense. Thanks to taking a chance, I finally knew where I was going and, most importantly, I was no longer travelling alone.

FINAL MESSAGES FROM THE REARVIEW MIRROR

As this was a difficult chapter for me to write (and experience), I have decided to end my chapter with a series of short messages to my younger self. Messages I wish were tucked in the glove box during my long road trip, ready to be read whenever I needed them. I gift these messages to you now in hopes that something may resonate.

To the Exhausted Student Hating Herself for Not Being Able to Finish Her PhD

Closing your laptop is not laziness and you are not wasting time. What you are feeling is your nervous system protecting you. You are not weak, difficult or broken. You are responding in a normal way for someone navigating amounts of trauma that would flatten most people. Just getting through the day is enough.

To the Pregnant Woman Wondering Why Everything Is so Hard

You are not naive for believing the advice you were given. You trusted people who meant well and wanted the best for you and your career, but your body and brain simply experience pregnancy differently. That difference is real, biological and worthy of care, not grit.

To the Mother at the Rest Stop, Drowning in Shame

You are not a failure for needing to stop, and you do not need fixing. You are still on the journey, even when the car is parked. You have not missed your opportunity; you are merely in the process of being rerouted. You will soon learn what kind of work your nervous system can sustain. Until then, keep pouring your love into your babies. When they are old enough, they will tell you just how grateful they are to you for being their advocates.

To the Newly Graduated PhD, Staring at the Empty Horizon

You are not unemployable, nor are you 'too much' or 'too late'. This silence is structural, not personal, and it will not be permanent. One day, you will start knocking down barriers and building roads that others have been quietly searching for, too.

And Finally, to the Girl with the Colour Coded Plan Who Just Wanted to Know Where She Was Going

You will get there. Not the destination you thought you were heading, but to one you help create. Soon you will look up and see clear signage, an open road and the longed-for travellers beside you. It is all going to be ok. You are going to be ok.

REFERENCES

Evans, A. D., & Lee, K. (2013). Emergence of lying in very young children. *Developmental Psychology*, *49*(10), 1958.

Grant, A., Jones, S., Williams, K., Leigh, J., & Brown, A. (2022). Autistic women's views and experiences of infant feeding: A systematic review of qualitative evidence. *Autism*, *26*(6), 1341–1352.

Hampton, S., Man, J., Allison, C., Aydin, E., Baron-Cohen, S., & Holt, R. (2022). A qualitative exploration of autistic mothers' experiences I: Pregnancy experiences. *Autism*, *27*(5), 1271–1282.

Maciver, D., Singh Roy, A., Johnston, L., Boilson, M., Curnow, E., Johnstone-Cooke, V., & Rutherford, M. (2025). Are we getting better at identifying and diagnosing neurodivergent girls and women? Insights into sex ratios and age of diagnosis from clinical population data in Scotland. *Autism*, *30*(2), 375–389.

Riordan, J., Timperley, S., O'Brien, C., Edwards, C., Murrihy, C., Harrison, M., McKay-Brown, L., & Mendus, A. (2024). Creating the conditions for inclusion: Investigating optimal physical spaces for supporting neurodivergent staff and postgraduate students. *Neurodiversity*, 2.

Spanò, G., Combs, D., Dwyer, P., Luongo, A., Parent-Johnson, W., & Edgin, J. (2024). Autism and sleep across development: Advancing research and treatment through co-production. *Neurodiversity*, 2.

Sundelin, H. E., Stephansson, O., Hultman, C. M., & Ludvigsson, J. F. (2018). Pregnancy outcomes in women with autism: A nationwide population-based cohort study. *Clinical Epidemiology*, *10*, 1817–1826.

Weir, E., Allison, C., Warrier, V., & Baron-Cohen, S. (2021). Increased prevalence of non-communicable physical health conditions among autistic adults. *Autism*, *25*(3), 681–694.

4

PEOPLE, POLITICS, POWER STRUCTURES AND POLITENESS: A CRASH COURSE IN SOCIAL DYNAMICS I WOULD RATHER HAVE AVOIDED

SARAH TIMPERLEY

The University of Melbourne, Australia

ABSTRACT

University courses can prepare aspiring academics well for the research side of academia but rarely, if ever, discuss the social aspects of academia that can make or break careers and people. This chapter examines the author's experiences with the social and political side of higher education as a neuro-divergent scholar who has not always excelled at figuring out the expectations and motivations of neurotypical colleagues. Despite generally being social and outgoing in her personal life, the author found that her simplistic expectations that colleagues would mostly be easy to collaborate with and put producing good research above egos and annoyances were dangerously wrong. The author explores her journey across three stories: being an undiagnosed PhD student grappling with social challenges stemming from her own anxiety and executive dysfunction; the disillusionment of working in a team that was ruthless in pursuit of power and prestige; and the painful realisation that missed social cues, poor attitudes towards neurodivergence and attempts to improve processes being misread as criticism led to unbearable workplace dynamics. Through the second and third stories, she discusses her choices to disclose and not disclose her ADHD and how the way neurodivergence is treated fed into her own feelings of isolation and uncertainty.

Keywords: Social dynamics; collaboration; neurodiversity; lived experience; social challenges

Source: Artwork by Melissa Vallence.
A Portrait of Sarah Timperley.

INTRODUCTION

Reflecting on my own experiences navigating the human side of academia has been incredibly difficult. Initially, I thought this would be a much simpler explanation of the things I have learnt; but as other authors dug deep into personal stories and our shared vision for the book evolved, I knew I would do both the other authors and the book as a whole a disservice as an editor by only touching the surface in my own chapter. Looking back at my own journey, I don't necessarily always like the person I've been, but I think a lot of us feel that at times.

This chapter chronicles my experiences learning to work with (or extract myself from) other researchers. From a naïve, undiagnosed PhD student causing stress and chaos with my own unexplained overwhelm to a jaded researcher,[1] this chapter chronicles the things I learnt about people and interacting with them that I was probably supposed to already know.

COMPLETING MY PHD: LETTING OVERWHELM AND ANXIETY TAKE THE WHEEL

I had no idea I was neurodivergent when I started my PhD. I was good at masking and completely in denial. I knew I wasn't exactly *mentally healthy*, but didn't think I deserved anyone's sympathy for anything, least of all my own pathetic inability to do basic human things. I managed to achieve academically despite incredible anxiety about not being able to do anything until the last minute[2] and had convinced myself that was enough.

I genuinely enjoyed research and still do. I love the feeling of thinking up a really good question and a solid way to answer it. But I can't deny part of the reason I did a PhD was also a deep sense of anxiety and dread about finding an actual job. I thought in an overly supervised setting, the days I languished in brain fog so thick I could barely string two thoughts together and my intense

---

[1]Whose overwhelm is now at least mostly explained.

[2]Which, paradoxically, I masked by acting overly relaxed about everything.

anxiety and frustration at doing basic administrative tasks would expose me as a useless worker and an intellectual fraud.

However, I had already done two research projects and enjoyed them. Supervisors rarely cared *when* work was done as long as it was done by the deadline; I could pull myself together enough to get data collection done, and could write great swathes right before a deadline to make up for the days my brain wouldn't work. What I didn't account for, though, was that my PhD project involved a lot of shared data collection with another PhD student.

The biggest issue, looking back, was that I really don't process details very well verbally. General things, like ideas and concepts, are fine. Specific things like names, dates, details and instructions? Forgotten immediately. Especially when I'm told multiple things at once. I recognise that now, but having previously had all my assignment instructions and dates written down and accessible online, I had no idea just how bad I would be at recalling these things in an environment where no one would write anything down for me, ever.

My first major faux pas was, predictably, missing a deadline that was given to me verbally. I think it was for printing booklets. I was told I'd missed this via my lab mate complaining that she had had to print them because they needed to go out. I had been convinced they were going out on a different day, but given my relationship with time, I assume she was right. Her telling off made me incredibly anxious, and my automatic reaction to anxiety was avoidance.

Every time she spoke to me after that, there was a tinge of annoyance to it. Like she shouldn't have to tell me things that she was telling me, though she had developed her own ways of working and organising things that she wanted me to follow. A cycle emerged; if I asked her something she thought I should know, or she'd told me before, she was annoyed. If I didn't ask, she would tell me off for doing things wrong. The more annoyed she got, the more avoidant and shut down I became, until I found it hard to process anything she said.[3]

[3]And of course, to the outside, this avoidance looked like I just didn't care.

She would tell me to do things, and I couldn't even process the words she was saying, let alone follow the instructions. I (barely) coped by figuring out how everything worked myself, but of course I was always doing things wrong because I wasn't following her instructions. The worst thing was, I understood why she was annoyed. She was right, I wasn't listening to her. I couldn't. A lot of the time I couldn't remember more than a vague haze of panic when I tried to recall what she'd said. I felt trapped and ashamed and like I could never do anything right. I'd like to say I figured out a way out of this, but actually she just left for a placement, and I was left alone to do all the data collection for both of our projects. In theory this should have been harder, but in practice, it was a huge relief. I put in place strategies that worked for me,[4] and the data was all collected.

During this period, I also made friends with a woman with an ADHD diagnosis. I had male friends who had been diagnosed, one of whom repeatedly told me I had ADHD and seemed very concerned that I kept brushing this suggestion off. Their ADHD just seemed different from what I experienced. This time, I saw so much of myself in my new friend that I couldn't ignore it anymore. I finally got a diagnosis, and the medication helped a lot. It didn't make me suddenly able to speak neurotypically, but it *did* help me organise myself enough to not feel a deep and constant existential panic that there was something I was forgetting. At this point, I thought that forgetting things and not following instructions had been the main cause of my issues with my lab mate – if I were better organised, I wouldn't have any more problems with colleagues. Right?

LAB POLITICS 1: PEOPLE ARE... DISINGENUOUS?

I've had a few jobs since my PhD, across a few different universities. I will obfuscate these and some of the details. Honestly, I would like to be done with many of the people involved, but also these stories shaped me so much that I can't write this chapter

[4]Mostly incredibly detailed spreadsheets and checklists.

without reflecting on them. I will say, however, that these stories are not my only experiences – between these episodes, I was lucky enough to work with people I got along really well with.

I don't know how I managed to be so incredibly naïve, but when I started the first job I will discuss (we'll call it 'Job A'), I had somehow held onto a belief that people doing the types of research I was doing must genuinely want to do what was best and make the world a better place. Some of them might not be super nice, but deep down they must care about the research they were doing. Otherwise, what was the point in doing it? Even though I had personally clashed with my PhD lab mate, she genuinely cared about her work and her community.

My experiences at the next workplace I discuss were almost the complete opposite of my PhD experience. I started Job A full of stimulants and optimism. I worked hard, I organised myself and I immediately wrote down any verbal instructions. I really enjoyed what I was working on, and felt like it was worthwhile. I was invited out socially by my new colleagues, and managed to mask well enough to stay in people's good graces. For the first few months, I hit the ground running and was so busy and trying so hard to be a good postdoc and please everyone that I didn't realise anything was amiss (at least not consciously). I had praise heaped on me and was shown the substantial benefits of being part of a well-funded team that took care of its own.

I didn't come out as neurodivergent, or as queer.[5] As well as things were going, I started getting hints pretty early on that this would be a bad idea. The 'in-group' was made up entirely of straight culturally homogenous able-bodied women of a certain social class,[6] and every now and then they would say things that set off alarm bells. Like the group leader telling us her friend's dyslexic son had 'ruined her life'. Or another woman constantly asking a new hire who was gay about how Grindr was going in a real 'Oh, a gay, how exotic!' sort of way (he quit after about three months).

---

[5]Coming out as bi feels weird at the best of times, and I'm still not sure if or when I should mention this most of the time.

[6]I was told multiple times that I should move house because my rental was in a 'bad' part of town, which seemed to just mean very slightly less white than the rest of the city.

I found over time that there were quite a few more diverse people around, but not in the 'in' group. These students (and occasionally colleagues) were shown off and featured prominently whenever something promotional happened, but never included in regular meetings. They would be wheeled out to be 'consulted' so that the group could say they had consulted a 'diverse cohort' and that their initiatives were 'culturally responsive', yet somehow all this consultation always ended with them doing exactly what had already been planned.

I can pinpoint what made me uncomfortable now,[7] but at the time I wasn't sure they were actually *bad*.[8] It clearly worried me enough not to come out, though. I feared they would wheel me out at events to say 'Oh look, we have a real live person with ADHD; everyone praise us for how WONDERFULLY inclusive we are!' while shutting me out of anything important. I know now this is *exactly* what would have happened.

Over time, it also became increasingly clear that I was being lied to. At first, I believed them because I didn't understand why they would lie to me. It didn't occur to me that they would be cutting corners in their research and ethics, taking credit and resources for other people's work, bullying other academics and students, and brushing off complaints about sexual harassment by one of their close collaborators *on purpose*. As things went on, however, I started asking questions. The evidence piled up. In fact, it got to a point where I had *so much* evidence of *so many* lies that it boggled my mind that they would just... continue to lie to me. Eventually, I realised that they were either fully gaslighting me or didn't actually expect me to *believe* the lies, just *pretend* to believe the lies because things were just easier for everyone that way.

It turned out I didn't need to come out as neurodivergent or queer to be shut out of the group. I just had to have ethical standards.[9]

---

[7]Mostly because I got confirmation from several of the people I saw this happening to that they absolutely were being exploited, and everyone knew it.
[8]Because, silly me, my field only contained good people. And they told everyone constantly about their principles and how wonderfully strengths-based and culturally responsive they were.
[9]Something shared by other neurodivergent people (Hartman & Hartman, 2024).

Through talking to pretty much anyone who had ever worked with them, I found out they were definitely terrible people and absolutely expected me to just... go along with whatever they wanted. OR ELSE. They constantly did similar things to everyone who came into contact with them, and people were terrified of them. I was working with vindictive, power-hungry bullies who would step over absolutely anyone if it meant furthering their own careers.

The worst part was that I had unknowingly been complicit in helping them take another academic's work; they had told me they were working with that academic, which had been a blatant lie that I should have verified but didn't know was necessary. I thought that we were looking at whether the benefits of a programme that an academic had developed were additive to a programme (targeting something different) the job A group had developed. Because that's an interesting research question and good to know. What I *hadn't* known was that this group saw the main reason for doing research as a means to package 'evidence-based' programmes to sell. And *of course* they intended to package and sell this other academic's programme as their own.

I can pinpoint exactly when it was decided that I was out of the group. The academic we were plagiarising from raised what was happening, and the job A in-group wanted me to say that it was all our work. They recorded the call, which consisted of an entire hour of them trying to gaslight and cajole me into saying we didn't copy anything.

I then solidified my exile when I repeatedly argued against removing tests that were incredibly important because they 'weren't showing significant results' so that we could pretend something was working based on the shaky evidence of a single sub-test that really wasn't supposed to be used on its own. I wasn't told I was off the project; I just stopped getting invited to meetings and was moved to work in a different building[10]. At that point I really didn't want to be part of it anymore anyway, but I still grieved for all the work I had put in when I thought we were doing something not completely reprehensible.

---

[10]I'm bad at taking hints, but even I noticed that one.

I was incredibly lucky during an otherwise unlucky time to have found a mentor outside of the group who had a strong sense of morality about ethical research practices.

I was warned by some that this person was 'using' me to execute a grudge against the academics who were causing harm, but I never felt this. I felt like I had been unknowingly complicit in some of the things I saw as immoral, and that *hurt,* and I *wanted* to do what I could to clear my conscience. She helped me to do that. She was a good mentor, and I saw her suffer politically from trying to do the right thing the same way I did. After I had left, I told her I was neurodivergent. It turned out that this person who was trained in the medical model and I once heard saying 'if children can't sit still they can't learn[11]' was actually one of the most empathetic and willing-to-learn people I've ever disclosed to.

The great thing about a postdoc is, unlike a PhD, you don't not get a PhD if you just quit. It wasn't as though my contract was going to be renewed anyway. I reached out to someone I had worked with previously to ask for a job. It was only a casual research assistant position, but at least I knew I liked the people I would be working with. And, because I had worked with them before, I didn't have to explain to strangers why I was quitting a post-doc. I filed a complaint, helped the people I could, and left the university (and the country). Another post-doc who worked with the group also quit around the same time, and a third was seriously considering it. At least I had a lot of confirmation that I wasn't the problem.

I know I would be much further along in my career if I had just... gone along with things. When I see other people's career trajectories, often launched by their first postdoc into publications and grants and a place in academia with a solid foundation, I do sometimes grieve. This experience killed my confidence, made me suspicious of opportunities that seemed 'too good', and worried that the vindictive and well-connected academic I had worked for would ruin my career if I accidently worked somewhere where she had influence.[12] I left with no publications, no grants, a shattered

[11]One of the reasons I hadn't initially disclosed to her.
[12]They knew about the formal complaint I laid.

sense of self, disillusionment about the integrity of academia and a hole in my CV (and my life) that I desperately wanted to forget.

I trauma-bonded[13] with colleagues and other academics who were also being bullied and lied to, but I haven't really stayed in touch despite really liking a lot of those people. I don't have much reason to visit, and my brain sort of wants to slide over that time and pretend it didn't happen as much as possible. I did go back once for a conference two years later and was stalked by my ex-boss.[14] Despite all this, I'm glad I stood up for myself, and I'm glad I left. I would rather not have a career at all than have become one of them.

LAB POLITICS 2: SOMETIMES I SUPPOSE I'M JUST ANNOYING

I'll skip forward to a different group I worked in, since the places I worked in between were pretty diverse and mostly non-hierarchical (that I noticed), and I got along well in those conditions.

By the time I started Job B, surely, I had it down. Be organised enough not to anger your colleagues. Keep an eye out for obvious red flags, like everyone who has ever worked with a group having nothing but loathing and disdain for them.

What follows is really the story of me annoying a lab head into hating me. On the one hand, it could have ruined my career (again), but on the other hand, it feels more light-hearted, being a more typical story of missed social cues than a sinister tale of attempted indoctrination into a group of well-funded and well-connected bullies.[15]

---

[13]I know it seems like I might be using the word trauma in an exaggerated way here, but I promise I'm not. These experiences were really genuinely traumatising to me and multiple people I worked with.

[14]After one of the in-group members happened to see me the first day, she came back with her boss the next day (even though she works in a different building across town), and they sat for about four hours at a café in the building hosting the conference that I had to constantly walk past. Neither of them was attending the conference. Ex-colleagues from that university confirmed that yes, they were stalking me. This was typical behaviour for them.

[15]I should note that while I can laugh about it now, at the time, what I'm about to describe was actually incredibly distressing.

In this case, too, everything started off well. People seemed to like this lab head.[16] She didn't openly put people down or repeatedly praise staff for their 'loyalty' during lab meetings (a staple of Job A). I was relaxed. Too relaxed. I let myself be myself, which was a mistake.

I know I spoke too much at lab meetings. I know this because the lab head would sort of huff or roll her eyes when I started talking. By the time I noticed this, it was probably too late. The problem was, my contributions were received positively by *most* of the group, so I didn't think I could be *that* annoying. I should have cared more that I was clearly annoying the most important person to *not* annoy.

I also messed up with the second most important person to not mess up with (we'll call her Person 2). My role was primarily data collection. I made the mistake of disclosing that I was neurodivergent to the person overseeing this data collection. I wasn't actually asking for anything, just explaining why I was working on a project around neurodiversity on days I didn't work for them.

From then on, this person spoke to me as though I was... slow? She would sort of speak slowly to me, and when she asked a question, if I didn't give her the answer she wanted, she would just keep repeating the question over and over again until I said whatever she wanted me to say. I would eventually give in and just give her the answer she wanted because I was done trying to talk to her. She clearly expected me to be incompetent and would assign me less work than others despite my repeated saying that I could do more. Then she would use the fact that I had gotten less work done (because she refused to assign me more) as evidence that I wasn't capable. Of course, when I repeatedly asked for the most basic accommodation imaginable (scheduling meetings with me instead of randomly accosting me when I was trying to do other things), this was ignored.

Towards the end of my time there, I told her I regretted telling her I have ADHD. She looked at me horrified and said, 'You didn't say you had ADHD, you told me you were neurodivergent'.

[16]Although I maybe should have noted that I seemed to be the only neurodivergent or queer person.

I suppose that whole time she thought that meant autistic. I'm pretty sure, now, that I *am* also autistic,[17] but I did find it darkly amusing that her treatment of me was based on bad stereotypes of the wrong thing.

Compounding these two issues was the real elephant, which was that I wouldn't let go of an issue with the data collection process that I thought needed to be addressed. I kept suggesting a way to improve our data reliability. I could see that Person 2 didn't understand it, and I didn't hold that against her at all; I was talking about a specific process with which I had a lot of experience. Nothing was done about the issue. This is where I really stepped my foot in it. Assuming that if everyone just understood the issue they would address it, I took all the data we had collected so far and did some statistics to demonstrate the problem. I included graphs. It was very detailed. This one I actually got yelled at for by the lab head. Apparently I was publicly criticising other people. I thought I was just trying to be helpful.

I got a bad performance review but also a contract extension, I assume because I needed to be punished, but also was actually quite good at my job.[18] I finally noticed all the little things that had been happening. People telling me they wanted me on a project, and then never hearing anything back. I had told Person 2 about a paper idea I had based on our data that wasn't in the plan and asked if she wanted to write it with me. She said she was too busy, but then later someone else was suddenly doing that paper, and I wasn't asked to be involved. In fact, ideas I expressed in meetings were frequently given to students or others without my involvement, despite me volunteering. It was the same pattern that happened after I declined to lie for the bullies. Then, I hadn't cared that much because by the time it started happening, I was already thinking about leaving (and I was already at rock bottom emotionally anyway, so there wasn't much further to go).

This time, I was really hurt. Other than what I thought was mild annoyance from the lab head and some bad stereotypes of

---

[17]I have been peer reviewed by so many autistic colleagues that at this point it just seems disrespectful to continue to ignore them.
[18]When not being actively sabotaged.

neurodivergence from Person 2, I had thought everything else was going well. Everyone except those two were happy with my work; I got along well with everyone else and thought I had been doing a good job. And then, like a burst dam, I started to see that everything was wrong. It was being yelled at that finally broke the dam for me – I'm really terrible at subtlety.

I think experience tends to compound; each time something goes horribly wrong, it feels like less of a fluke and more of a pattern. And this time, I was the only one. Other times, other places, when I was treated badly, everyone was treated badly. Here I was completely alone. Everyone else loved the lab. Everyone else was normal.

The other project I was on saved me. I was interviewing other neurodivergent staff about their experiences. It turned out I wasn't the only one – the things I had been experiencing were reflected across a dozen other stories. I think that's what I want to give others with this book. To know that things can be really hard sometimes, but none of us are alone in this.

I know it seems silly, but I hadn't really thought about how being neurodivergent impacted me *socially*. I kind of just shrugged that side of things off because I *thought* I was fine with people because I have great friends (...who are mostly also neurodivergent). I'm not, I figured out. I was supposed to be deferring to those above me, and instead I was giving my opinions, repeatedly, unwantedly, with statistical evidence. I was acting above my station and hadn't even noticed there was a station. I didn't get hints to drop things. At the time, I happened across a paper by Finke and Dunn (2023), in which they described violations of neurotypical social expectations as a reason for neurodivergent exclusion. This phrasing helped me frame my own experiences at the time; I can see that I was constantly violating social expectations. I wish they had just talked to me about it instead of punishing me for things I wasn't really aware of, but here we are.

I was lucky enough to be pulled out of this into neurodiversity research. My own experiences, and those I hear over and over from others, have lit something inside me (other than just anxiety, this time). The models of ADHD and autism (and a whole lot of other things) that still influence so many people's understanding today were designed to 'deal with' us,[19] not help us (Kapp, 2019). No one told me what to expect in the workplace, how to advocate for myself (or even that I would need to), or that other people were going through the same things, unseen, all around me. There are amazing people in the field shedding light on this, and I am incredibly grateful for this. But that light took a long time to filter down to me, because it was so drowned out by research about deficits written by researchers who see us as, at best, interesting mistakes. The light certainly hadn't touched some of my colleagues or the services I tried to access for help. The solace I found was in my community, and now that I've found it, I'm not letting go.

I don't mean for this piece to be a complaint, but rather a love letter to everyone who, like me, has struggled to make sense of the social climate around them. Who've tried their best but still messed up; whose trust in others has been broken; who've been sidelined because of social dynamics that seem to make no sense. I've learned a lot, mostly through messing up, and I hope those stories help others to avoid similar situations (or at least feel less alone in them). I know not everyone has this luxury, but the best piece of advice I can give is to find people who accept you. Find people you can argue with and figure things out[20] without it ruining your career. Because everyone should be allowed to grow from our mistakes, and none of us should be made to feel like being ourselves is inherently wrong.

REFERENCES

Finke, E. H., & Dunn, D. H. (2023). Neurodiversity and double empathy: Can empathy disconnects be mitigated to support autistic belonging?. *Disability & Society*, *0*(0), 1–24. https://doi.org/10.1080/09687599.2023.2295802

[19]Or at least deal with the stereotypically presenting assigned-male-at-birth children version of us.

[20]Argue about things like best research methods and not sending emails at three AM, not things like whether you are a 'burden on society'.

Hartman, L., & Hartman, B. (2024). An ethical advantage of autistic employees in the workplace. *Frontiers in Psychology*, *15*, 1364691. https://doi.org/10.3389/fpsyg.2024.1364691

Kapp, S. K. (2019). How social deficit models exacerbate the medical model: Autism as case in point. *Autism Policy & Practice*, *2*(1), 3–28. https://openaccessautism.org/index.php/app/article/view/16

5

IMPOSTER SYNDROME AS A NEURODIVERGENT EARLY CAREER ACADEMIC

JENNY MAI PHAN

George Mason University, USA

ABSTRACT

This chapter explores the unique manifestations of imposter syndrome among neurodivergent early-career scholars in academia, challenging framings that locate the problem within individual psychology. Drawing from lived experience as an autistic researcher and scholarly literature on neurodiversity, stigma and academic culture, Jenny examines how imposter syndrome emerges at the intersection of neurodivergent ways of being and institutional structures designed around neurotypical norms. The chapter identifies three primary sources of imposter syndrome: self-imposed perceptions from comparisons with neurotypical peers and internalised ableism; externally imposed pressures through well-meaning but neurotypical-centric professional development advice and mentorship; and institutionally mandated practices that conflict with neurodivergent cognitive styles and sensory needs. These challenges are further compounded for neurodivergent researchers with multiple marginalised identities. Rather than treating imposter syndrome as an individual deficit, Jenny reframes it as a rational response to systemic exclusion, exploring how academia's hidden curriculum and infantilisation of autistic individuals contribute to persistent feelings of fraudulence among competent neurodivergent scholars.

Keywords: Neurodiversity; imposter syndrome; academic culture; cultural competemility; intersectionality

Source: Artwork by Olivia Dang.
A Portrait of Jenny Mai Phan.

INTRODUCTION

Academia operates on unspoken rules – a hidden curriculum that dictates everything from how to network at conferences to what constitutes 'productive' work habits. For neurodivergent early career researchers, navigating these unstated expectations can feel like decoding a foreign language without a dictionary. When our brain processes information differently, when sensory environments overwhelm us and when social communication follows patterns that diverge from institutional norms, the persistent question emerges: Am I not good enough, or is the system not designed for people like me?

Here, imposter syndrome takes root – not merely as individual self-doubt, but as a rational response to structural barriers that fail to recognise neurodivergent ways of being as equally valid approaches to scholarship.

Imposter syndrome, characterised by persistent feelings of being a fraud despite evident success, disproportionately affects researchers from marginalised backgrounds (Posselt, 2020). For neurodivergent academics, these feelings are compounded by the internalisation of stigma associated with autism and other neurodivergences, leading to decreased self-esteem, increased mental health problems and reluctance to seek accommodations (Botha et al., 2022).

This chapter draws from my lived experience as an autistic researcher navigating academic spaces from undergraduate studies through an assistant professorship, alongside scholarly literature on neurodiversity, stigma and academic culture. I write as someone who entered higher education without family guidance, who discovered my autism diagnosis only after recognising features in my own children and who has spent a decade advocating for more inclusive research practices while simultaneously questioning whether academia will accept me.

THE HIDDEN CURRICULUM AND OTHERING OF NEURODIVERGENT SCHOLARS

Academic institutions operate on assumptions of neurotypicality. Academia's hidden curriculum – unspoken rules and norms that, when violated, lead to punishment or othering – presents particular challenges for neurodivergent scholars (Cage & Howes, 2020; Jones, 2023). These norms pervade every level of academic life: maintaining eye contact during presentations, informal networking at social events, assuming identical information processing and a premium placed on rapid verbal responses.

Autistic people often struggle with self-identity due to societal perceptions of autism as a deficit (Botha & Gillespie-Lynch, 2022). This deficit framing permeates academic culture. When our natural communication style, information processing, or work patterns differ from institutional norms, we face a constant choice: mask my differences or risk being perceived as unprofessional, incompetent or difficult.

SOURCES OF IMPOSTER SYNDROME: SELF-IMPOSED, EXTERNALLY IMPOSED, AND INSTITUTIONALLY MANDATED

Imposter syndrome in neurodivergent academics stems from multiple, often interconnected sources. Understanding these sources is essential for addressing not just individual feelings of inadequacy but also the systemic barriers that generate them.

Self-Imposed Perceptions

Neurodivergent people of colour, who must code-switch and conceal neurodivergent features to avoid discrimination based on multiple identities, often resort to 'triple masking'. As a Vietnamese American woman from a refugee family background, I found myself constantly calibrating: Was I being perceived as too quiet because of my autism, my cultural background or my gender? Did my request for written agendas signal weakness or legitimate accommodation needs?

Masking, camouflaging or code-switching to blend in with neurotypical peers often comes at the expense of psychological well-being and sense of identity. Yet the alternative – being visibly different – carries its own risks. I postponed my autism diagnosis disclosure for months, fearing it would confirm suspicions that I wasn't 'faculty material'.

The comparisons are relentless. Other academics seem to network effortlessly, write prolifically and juggle multiple projects without visible strain. When my brain requires more recovery time after social interaction, when I need detailed written and paced instructions rather than verbal handoffs, when I hyperfocus productively on one project but struggle with rapid task-switching or multi-tasking, it's easy to interpret these differences as deficits. My overcompensating usually results in immediate or same-day burnout; therefore, I need longer recovery times.

Externally Imposed Through Well-Meaning Advice

Professional development workshops and training often employ methods that fail to account for neurodivergent learning and communication needs (Clouder et al., 2020; Jones, 2023). I've attended countless productivity workshops advocating techniques that fundamentally conflict with how my neurodivergence works: 'Just start writing, even if it's bad!' (when executive function challenges make initiating tasks without structure nearly impossible), 'Network with five new people at every conference!' (when managing one meaningful conversation exhausts my social energy reserves), 'Keep your workspace minimal and organised!' (when visual cues and organised chaos represent my external memory system). This advice isn't malicious – it's neurotypical-centric. When these strategies inevitably fail for neurodivergent academics, we internalise that failure as personal inadequacy rather than recognising the mismatch between method and neurology.

Mentors, too, can unintentionally reinforce imposter feelings. When accommodations are framed as burdensome exceptions rather than normalised, flexible practices of care, they reinforce ableist assumptions about productivity. I recall a senior colleague suggesting I 'just push through' sensory overwhelm during a multi-day conference, framing accommodation as weakness rather than necessity. Pushing through sensory overload has resulted in hiding in my hotel room the next full day to recover. I lose out on networking opportunities (e.g., lunches, dinners) and professional development when I hide in my room to recover for ~12–24 hours while at a conference. The advice to push through was well-meaning and carried the undertone that conferencing can cause sensory overwhelm for many people. However, my sensory overload leads to mental, cognitive and physical impairments for the subsequent 12+ hours, which is not common among other attendees. A paced and structured approach would improve my participation.

Institutionally Mandated Practices

Perhaps the most insidious source of imposter syndrome emerges when institutions mandate practices that fundamentally conflict with neurodivergent ways of working, then pathologise our struggle to comply.

In community and healthcare settings, the needs of autistic individuals are often overlooked, with professionals dismissing symptoms or concerns as merely behavioural issues rather than legitimate needs (Tint & Weiss, 2018). This dismissal extends to academic settings. For example, requesting a quiet workspace away from open office plans might be met with suggestions that our need is excessive accommodation rather than a reasonable adjustment for sensory processing differences (Jones, 2023; Mellifont, 2023).

Existing disability accommodation systems often rely on formal disclosure processes that are not only bureaucratic but also risky, as disclosure can trigger stigma or career penalties (Brown & Leigh, 2018; Mellifont, 2023). The burden falls entirely on neurodivergent individuals to disclose, document, request and often repeatedly justify our needs – a process demanding significant executive function, self-advocacy capacity and emotional labour. Potentially, accommodation requests can be awkward interactions with supervisors or mentors (Jones, 2023; Spier & Natalier, 2023).

Even when accommodations are technically available, they're frequently inadequate (Jones, 2023; Spier & Natalier, 2023); for instance, navigating the human resources system to submit forms and documents is difficult to access. Educational and community service settings often show an absence of cultural competemility (Hotez et al., 2024) – a concept I will discuss below, contributing to high push-out rates for autistic adults (Cage & Howes, 2020). The accommodation might be granted (i.e., quieter workspace), but the culture remains unchanged. Colleagues still schedule impromptu verbal meetings, assume everyone processes information identically, and reward those who perform productively in neurotypical, legible ways.

INFANTILISING NEURODIVERGENCE

One particularly insidious contributor to imposter syndrome among neurodivergent academics is infantilisation – the practice of treating someone as much younger than their age in ways that undermine their autonomy, intelligence, and capabilities (Stevenson et al., 2011). In academic settings, infantilisation manifests when neurodivergent scholars' professional judgement is questioned, their expertise doubted or their capacity for independent decision-making undermined, despite holding the same credentials and positions as neurotypical colleagues.

Biases in society reflect widespread infantilisation of autistic individuals, perpetuating systemic inequalities by treating autistic people based on perceived rather than actual competence (Hotez et al., 2023). Infantilisation in academic contexts takes multiple forms, each contributing to feelings of fraudulence even among accomplished neurodivergent scholars.

A particularly common manifestation of infantilisation occurs when neurodivergent scholars' professional process is misinterpreted as incompetence. I have experienced this in professional writing contexts. Like many academics, I follow conventional writing pedagogy – generate ideas first, refine later. I would bring draft materials to writing sessions with individuals who know my writing background, expecting substantive discussions: How should key arguments be framed? What priorities should be emphasised? What strategies would strengthen the overall narrative? Instead, these sessions would consistently focus on surface-level corrections – line-by-line corrections of syntax, punctuation and sentence structure – the very elements I had deliberately deprioritised in early drafts to focus on conceptual development. The implicit message became clear: The writing was so fundamentally deficient that we couldn't address strategic questions until basic composition issues were resolved.

This pattern reflects a broader dynamic of infantilisation. Rather than being treated as a credentialled scholar who understood writing as an iterative process, I was approached as someone needing remedial instruction. The irony was sharp, given my background: I had experience as a writing consultant, had taught university courses, and had published peer-reviewed articles. Yet deliberately rough early drafts were interpreted as evidence of inability to write professionally.

My responses to this dynamic revealed the toll of infantilisation. I became silent during sessions, offering only minimal acknowledgements: 'I'll do better'. This wasn't professional dialogue between colleagues; it was the dynamic of a student being corrected by a teacher – or more accurately, a child being corrected by an adult. I internalised the message that bringing imperfect drafts was wasting others' time, that I should arrive with polished prose rather than ideas needing development.

What made this experience particularly damaging was the impossibility of the standard being applied. The purpose of early professional development should be exploring content and strategy when both parties' cognitive resources are fresh – not copyediting, which can happen at later stages. By focusing relentlessly on surface-level errors in preliminary drafts, the mentorship communicated was that my fundamental capability as a writer was in question.

This dynamic is especially fraught for neurodivergent scholars from multilingual backgrounds or those with language-based processing differences. When English is not our first language, or when dysgraphia affects written output, or when executive function challenges mean editing happens in distinct phases rather than simultaneously with drafting, the expectation of consistently polished prose in all contexts becomes another hurdle to clear before being treated as a professional peer.

The impact on imposter syndrome was significant. If experienced professionals in my field could not see past surface errors to engage with substantive ideas, perhaps my ideas were not substantive enough to merit attention. Perhaps I really didn't belong in spaces where polished academic prose was the entry fee for being taken seriously. Perhaps my multi-stage writing process – messy drafting followed by extensive revision – was evidence of inadequacy rather than a valid approach used by many successful academics.

Paired with the mental strain of this experience, I noticed a significant increase in frequency and intensity of dysregulated stimming (or repetitive, restricted behaviours, thoughts or stereotypies) during this period. I was unable to control the dysregulated stimming in public when I usually had enough capacity to self-regulate enough to find a safe space to stim privately. My body was signalling distress even when I couldn't yet fully articulate the source.

Only much later did I recognise this as infantilisation rather than appropriate professional development. The approach may have been well-intentioned, perhaps genuinely aimed at helping me improve. But the effect was to position me as someone needing basic skills instruction rather than professional development, someone whose process couldn't be trusted, and someone who wasn't yet ready for substantive strategic guidance. I also faced the dilemma of whether disclosure would have changed the dynamic: Did my neurodivergence influence how my work was perceived?

What would have looked different? An approach that presumed competence might have said: 'I see you're still developing the prose – that's fine for this stage. Let's focus on whether your aims are compelling and how you're positioning your key points'. This treats rough drafts as normal parts of the writing process, not as evidence requiring remediation before substantive work can begin. If writing support were genuinely needed, a mentor could point out specific resources – 'After a couple of our writing sessions, I notice some recurring patterns with comma usage; here's a style guide that might help' – without derailing the entire session to grammar instruction.

The lesson for institutions and mentors: neurodivergent scholars may have different processes that don't always look like neurotypical professional norms. Someone who thinks best by writing messy drafts and revising extensively isn't less competent than someone who crafts polished sentences on the first pass – they're employing a different but equally valid approach. Treating process differences as deficits requiring correction is infantilisation, and it directly contributes to the imposter syndrome that neurodivergent academics struggle to overcome.

INTERSECTIONALITY: COMPOUNDED MARGINALISATION

Autistic individuals with multiple marginalised intersectional identities often experience heightened minority stress and greater negative health outcomes and unmet healthcare needs (Hotez et al., 2023, 2024). The intersection of neurodivergence with race, ethnicity, gender and other marginalised identities creates multiplicative rather than additive challenges (Phan et al., 2025).

This dynamic places neurodivergent ethnic minorities at a disadvantage in critical settings, limiting access to opportunities and impeding professional advancement. As a Vietnamese American woman growing up in a low-income, refugee family background, I've often been unable to determine whether barriers stem from racism, ableism, sexism, classism or their intersection. Was I passed over for opportunities because of my communication style, my race, my gender, my junior status or all of these factors compounding? In the infantilisation example above, I faced an additional layer of uncertainty: Should I have shared that English was my second language or that I was minimally verbal in early childhood? Would that explanation have shifted how my writing process was perceived, or would it have simply added another deficit to justify?

Multiple marginalised identities create unique challenges in disclosure. Autistic individuals with intersecting identities face compounded discrimination and may fear stigma from multiple directions (Phan et al., 2025). I often struggle with whether to disclose my autism diagnosis, partly because I already felt hyper-visible as one of the few Asian women in my field – adding another marginalised identity felt like painting an even larger target.

Before I recognised my own autism, I had already learned how society treats Asian women – through both observation and direct experience. An older male colleague once asked me, with what seemed like genuine curiosity: 'How does it feel to be the only Asian, Asian woman on this committee?' The question itself revealed my hypervisibility; I was not simply a committee member but a marked presence, notable for my difference.

The hypervisibility of my race and gender also made me a target for what I can only describe as ideological probing. As a graduate student, a senior professor – a White man in a position of considerable power over my academic trajectory – casually asked me directly: 'Do you believe that microaggression is a valid concept?'

At the time, I didn't fully register the layers of problematic dynamics in this interaction. Like many autistic people, I tend to process social interactions literally in the moment, only recognising the implicit meanings, power dynamics, and – isms much later – sometimes after replaying the scenario in my mind repeatedly (itself an autistic feature), sometimes only after someone else points out what happened when I recount the experience. This delayed recognition is characteristic of how many autistic people process social information, particularly interactions laden with subtext and power dynamics that aren't explicitly stated.

Only later did I unpack what was actually happening: A person in power questioning the legitimacy of a framework designed to name the very dynamics we were enacting. A White man asking an Asian woman whether her experiences of subtle discrimination were 'real'. The implicit message was that my perceptions of marginalisation were up for debate, requiring validation from those who held institutional authority. And all of this happened while I was a student dependent on this individual's support for my degree completion and career advancement.

I don't recall my exact response, but I remember the careful calibration required – how to acknowledge the validity of my own lived experience without seeming 'too sensitive', how to educate without appearing confrontational, how to maintain the relationship I needed for professional survival. This is the exhausting calculus that scholars with multiple marginalised identities perform constantly: simultaneously defending the legitimacy of our experiences while trying not to be marked as 'difficult' or 'divisive'.

This delayed recognition of discrimination adds another dimension to imposter syndrome for neurodivergent scholars from marginalised backgrounds. At the moment, I often don't recognise when I'm being treated unfairly due to my race, gender, or neurodivergence – I simply internalise the interaction as evidence that I've done something wrong, that I'm not good enough, that I don't belong. The doubt comes first; the understanding that the situation was discriminatory comes later, if at all. By then, I've already absorbed the message of inadequacy, already questioned my own competence, already wondered if I'm imagining things when I finally do recognise the pattern.

This creates a particularly vicious cycle: I experience discrimination but don't recognise it as such at the moment. I blame myself instead. Later – sometimes weeks or months later – I realise what actually happened. But by then, I've already reinforced my own imposter syndrome, already told myself I need to 'do better', already adjusted my behaviour to try to prevent similar interactions. The damage is done before I can even name it.

With the marginalisation of the intersection of race and gender already operating in ways I often didn't immediately recognise, I feared disclosing autism – an invisible disability – would either be dismissed ('You don't look autistic') or would confirm suspicions that I didn't truly belong in academia. This is the particular bind of intersectional invisibility that many neurodivergent scholars from marginalised backgrounds face. We are simultaneously too visible (marked by race, gender, accent and age) and invisible (our neurodivergence unrecognised, our specific needs unseen, the discrimination we face not immediately apparent even to ourselves). Disclosure of autism risks is shifting from invisible to hypervisible along yet another axis of difference, inviting additional scrutiny and scepticism. When you're already navigating assumptions about your competence based on race and gender – when even the concept of microaggression is presented as debatable – adding neurodivergence to that calculus can feel like volunteering for compounded marginalisation (Botha & Gillespie-Lynch, 2022).

When people in positions of power explicitly question the validity of frameworks meant to name marginalisation, it deepens the self-doubt – especially when I don't immediately recognise that questioning as itself a form of marginalisation. If microaggressions aren't 'real', then perhaps I'm imagining the ways my race affects how I'm treated. If I'm imagining that, perhaps I'm also imagining the infantilisation, the dismissiveness, the exclusion. Perhaps the problem really is just me – my writing, my communication style, my inability to network 'correctly', my tendency to misinterpret social situations. This is how imposter syndrome becomes entangled with gaslighting: When the structures that marginalise us simultaneously deny that marginalisation exists, and when our own neurodivergent social processing means we often don't recognise the marginalisation until well after we've already internalised the blame.

CULTURAL COMPETEMILITY

Cultural competemility – a synergistic blend of cultural competence and humility – requires support providers to maintain both an attitude and lens of cultural competence and humility as they engage in cultural encounters, obtain cultural knowledge, demonstrate cultural skill, and become culturally aware of their own biases and 'isms' (Hotez et al., 2024). This framework, while developed for healthcare, applies equally to academic institutions and directly addresses the sources of imposter syndrome outlined throughout this chapter.

Had my professional writing sessions been grounded in cultural competemility, the experience would have looked fundamentally different. A culturally competent approach would have involved asking about my writing process rather than assuming deficiency, recognising that executive function differences might mean I organise tasks in distinct phases and adapting mentorship to my needs rather than imposing a single 'correct' approach. The outcome wouldn't just be better writing – it would be a relationship where I felt valued as a professional peer rather than infantilised as someone needing remediation.

Some institutions are already implementing cultural competemility approaches. The journal *Autism in Adulthood* requires at least one autistic reviewer per paper, including non-academic reviewers who are compensated (Tan et al., 2025). The Framework for Open and Reproducible Research Training (FORRT) Neurodiversity Team, of which I am a member, uses asynchronous communication, provides materials in advance and treats accommodations as collaborative rather than administrative (Phan et al., 2025).

For academic settings, cultural competemility means:

- Trusting neurodivergent scholars' judgement about their needs and processes;
- Making accessibility standard rather than exceptional – lecture recordings, multiple communication modes (e.g., transcripts, screen reader, texts, visual descriptions), flexible work arrangements offered to all;
- Treating environmental adjustments as routine rather than burdensome exceptions
- Including neurodivergent voices in institutional decision-making, not just as consultants but as equal partners;
- Challenging biases through authentic collaboration with autistic individuals in research co-design.

For me, if these were practiced, this would mean I would not have had to risk disclosure and rejection by requesting a place away from open-plan work environments; the institution would recognise that open-plan spaces are a barrier to many people and have lower sensory environments available already and would have the humility to know that I, not them, am the expert in my own needs.

Cultural competemility directly addresses imposter syndrome by validating neurodivergent ways of being and working. When institutions presume competence, respect diverse processes and proactively create accessible environments, neurodivergent scholars receive consistent external messages that we belong, that our approaches are legitimate and that our differences are variations rather than deficits.

MOVING FORWARD: INDIVIDUAL STRATEGIES AND COLLECTIVE ACTION

I don't have all the answers. What I offer in this chapter is one autistic researcher's experience navigating academia – the barriers I've encountered, the patterns I've recognized (often belatedly) and the strategies I've developed. Your experience may differ. The sources of our imposter syndrome may be unique to our discipline, our institution and our intersecting identities. But perhaps in sharing my story, you'll recognise pieces of your own. Perhaps you'll feel less alone.

While we work towards structural change, neurodivergent early career academics need strategies for navigating existing systems.

Reframing 'Deficit' as 'Difference'

When we notice ourselves thinking 'my work process is slow', try 'I work at a different pace – producing thorough rather than rushed work'. This isn't denying real challenges; it's refusing to internalise ableist narratives about what's 'normal'.

Building Neurodivergent Community

Seek out other neurodivergent academics. Shared experiences validate what feels isolating when you're the only one. Community connectedness has important implications for well-being and coping with minority stress (Botha et al., 2022).

Strategic Disclosure

Consider who needs to know, what they need to know, when and what risks and benefits exist. There's no universally right answer – only what feels safest and most useful in our specific context.

Documenting Your Contributions

Because neurodivergent work patterns may not be visible in neurotypical-legible ways, keep records of accomplishments, contributions and impacts. This serves both for evaluation processes and for countering imposter syndrome in our own minds.

Seeking Neurodivergent-Affirming Mentorship

Find mentors who understand neurodivergent experiences or are willing to learn – people who presume competence, respect your process and advocate for systemic change alongside you.

But individual strategies aren't enough. We need collective action requiring institutional transformation: Universal Design as default, cultural competemility training for all faculty and staff, participatory governance that includes neurodivergent voices and recognition that neurodivergent scholarship enriches rather than detracts from academic quality.

CONCLUSION

Imposter syndrome in neurodivergent early-career academics isn't primarily a psychological problem requiring individual intervention. It's a rational response to institutional structures that weren't designed for neurodivergent people and haven't been sufficiently reformed to include us.

The infantilisation I experienced in professional writing sessions, the delayed recognition of microaggressions that left me blaming myself before understanding the discrimination, the hypervisibility as an Asian woman paired with the invisibility of my neurodivergent needs – these aren't separate challenges. They're interconnected manifestations of systems that presume neurotypicality, whiteness, maleness and able-bodiedness as default. When you don't fit those presumptions, imposter syndrome becomes the internalisation of repeated external messages that you don't quite belong.

When I feel like an imposter now, I ask myself: Am I actually inadequate, or is the system measuring me against neurotypical norms? Usually, it's the latter. I say this because I put in the work to conform and to assimilate all my life, yet the imposter feeling persists. My research productivity and scholarly contributions are genuine – they just don't always look the way academic culture expects.

The goal isn't eliminating all self-doubt; some reflection drives growth. Rather, it's distinguishing between useful self-reflection and internalised ableism, between genuine areas for development and structural barriers masquerading as personal failure. It's recognising that my multi-stage writing process, my need for recovery time after social interaction and my difficulty recognising discrimination in the moment – these aren't deficits. They're features of neurodivergent ways of being that need accommodation and respect.

I don't know if sharing my experience will change academia. I don't know if the cultural competemility framework will be widely adopted, if Universal Design will become standard or if the hidden curriculum will become explicit. What I do know is that writing this chapter has helped me understand my own imposter syndrome differently – not as personal failure but as structural problems. And if one neurodivergent early-career academic reads this and thinks 'I'm not alone in this', then perhaps that's enough for now.

REFERENCES

Botha, M., Dibb, B., & Frost, D. M. (2022). "Autism is me": An investigation of how autistic individuals make sense of autism and stigma. *Disability & Society*, *37*(3), 427–453. https://doi.org/10.1080/09687599.2020.1822782

Botha, M., & Gillespie-Lynch, K. (2022). Come as you are: Examining autistic identity development and the neurodiversity movement through an intersectional lens. *Human Development*, *66*(2), 93–112. https://doi.org/10.1159/000524123

Brown, N., & Leigh, J. (2018). Ableism in academia: Where are the disabled and ill academics? *Disability & Society*, *33*(6), 985–989. https://doi.org/10.1080/09687599.2018.1455627

Cage, E., & Howes, J. (2020). Dropping out and moving on: A qualitative study of autistic people's experiences of university. *Autism*, *24*(7), 1664–1675. https://doi.org/10.1177/1362361320918750

Clouder, L., Karakus, M., Cinotti, A., Ferreyra, M. V., Fierros, G. A., & Rojo, P. (2020). Neurodiversity in higher education: A narrative synthesis. *Higher Education*, *80*(4), 757–778. https://doi.org/10.1007/s10734-020-00513-6

Hotez, E., Phan, J. M., & Truong, D. M. (2024). Addressing stigma-related health disparities for autistic individuals through cultural competemility: Insights from research and lived experience. *Current Psychiatry Reports*, *26*(12), 761–770. https://doi.org/10.1007/s11920-024-01551-y

Hotez, E., Rava, J., Russ, S., Ware, A., & Halfon, N. (2023). Using a life course health development framework to combat stigma-related health disparities for individuals with intellectual and/or developmental disability (I/DD). *Current Problems in Pediatric and Adolescent Health Care*, *53*(5), 101433. https://doi.org/10.1016/j.cppeds.2023.101433

Jones, S. C. (2023). Autistics working in academia: What are the barriers and facilitators? *Autism*, *27*(3), 822–831. https://doi.org/10.1177/13623613221118158

Mellifont, D. (2023). Ableist ivory towers: A narrative review informing about the lived experiences of neurodivergent staff in contemporary higher education. *Disability & Society*, *38*(5), 865–886. https://doi.org/10.1080/09687599.2021.1965547

Phan, J. M., Middleton, S. L., Azevedo, F., Iley, B. J., Grose-Hodge, M., Tyler, S. L., Kapp, S. K., Yeung, S. K., Shaw, J. J., Hartmann, H., & Forrt (2025). Bridging neurodiversity and open scholarship: How shared values can guide best practices for research integrity, social justice, and principled education. *Journal of Social Issues*, *81*(4), e70035. https://doi.org/10.1111/josi.70035

Posselt, J. R. (2020). *Equity in science: Representation, culture, and the dynamics of change in graduate education*. Stanford University Press.

Spier, J., & Natalier, K. (2023). Reasonable adjustments? Disabled research higher degree students' strategies for managing their candidature in an Australian university. *Disability & Society*, *38*(8), 1365–1386. https://doi.org/10.1080/09687599.2021.1997718

Stevenson, J. L., Harp, B., & Gernsbacher, M. A. (2011). Infantilizing autism. *Disability Studies Quarterly*, *31*(3). https://doi.org/10.18061/dsq.v31i3.1675

Tan, D. W., Crane, L., Haar, T., Heyworth, M., Poulsen, R., & Pellicano, E. (2025). Reporting community involvement in autism research: Findings from the journal Autism. *Autism*, *29*(2), 490–503. https://doi.org/10.1177/13623613241275263

Tint, A., & Weiss, J. A. (2018). A qualitative study of the service experiences of women with autism spectrum disorder. *Autism*, *22*(8), 928–937. https://doi.org/10.1177/1362361317702561

6

BURNOUT IN ENVIRONMENTS SHAPED BY SCARCITY

KATHRYN E RINGLAND

University of California, Santa Cruz, USA

ABSTRACT

This chapter is a field report from inside academic burnout. Written by a neurodivergent scholar still living within exhaustion, it blends memoir, critique and manifesto to examine how the university consumes care, creativity and time – especially from disabled and neurodivergent faculty. Burnout here is framed not as an individual failure but as a structural condition, one produced by ableist norms of productivity, constant masking and the invisible labour of mentoring, accessibility and emotional caretaking. Through personal reflection and collective examples from the author's own research group, the Misfit Lab, the chapter explores how a culture of care can emerge within systems that reward endurance over empathy. Drawing on disability studies and lived experience, it traces the slow erosion of energy, the persistence of community and the small acts of resistance that make survival possible. Rather than promising recovery, the essay offers clarity: burnout as embodied knowledge as evidence of what needs to change. It closes with a manifesto for rebuilding academia around care instead of collapse.

Keywords: Burnout; neurodivergence; disability; academia; survival

Source: Artwork by Melissa Vallence.
A Portrait of Kathryn E Ringland.

THE FIRE YOU DON'T SEE

I don't think it's hyperbolic to write: this is one of the hardest essays I've had to write. Looking at my calendar, we are 12 days past the original deadline for this chapter. I asked for an extension because of illness – it's fall here in my part of the world, and cold season is upon us. I've had innumerable conversations with friends, family and colleagues about this piece. Those conversations reminded me how rarely we talk about burnout while it's happening. Most of us only narrate it in past tense, once we've survived enough to sound wise.

This chapter is meant to offer perspective – strategies, reflections, maybe even hope – for surviving and thriving in academia as a burnt-out neurodivergent scholar. What I have instead are fragments. Exhaustion, cynicism, stubborn love for my students and a refusal to look away from what this job does to us.

The emails keep arriving anyway. Another set of student projects waits to be graded. There's a conference deadline looming. I keep toggling between this document and my inbox, the cursor blinking like a metronome of guilt. The emotional labour of holding space for students, especially in hard times, is real and somehow never counted in the calculus of productivity. Even now, my body runs on fumes – caffeine, cortisol and a vague sense of obligation.

Academia rewards output, not honesty. We are expected to metabolise our pain into productivity, to turn breakdown into insight. When I first agreed to write this chapter, I imagined I'd have something insightful to say about recovery, how I clawed my way back, maybe even found balance. Instead, I'm still in the middle of the fire, writing from the ashes because deadlines don't care if you're smouldering.

I'm writing about burnout while still in it. The irony is not lost on me.

For neurodivergent academics, burnout isn't a temporary detour. It's the terrain itself. Each term we patch the bridge beneath our own feet, hoping it holds long enough to carry us to something gentler. My nervous system doesn't reset when the term ends. It just idles louder.

So this isn't a story about overcoming. It's a field report from inside the exhaustion. A chronicle of what it means to keep teaching, mentoring and caring while your own edges are fraying. Writing this is my act of resistance, or maybe just an act of honesty and self-care.

THE LONG BURN

Burnout didn't arrive like a lightning strike. It crept in quietly, the way exhaustion masquerades as normalcy. One term blurred into the next, each filled with small compromises and invisible injuries. I used to imagine burnout as a collapse – one spectacular failure that forced you to stop. But mine has been a long erosion, a kind of death by a 1,000 papercuts. It didn't happen all at once. It just kept happening until I realised I no longer remembered what it felt like to be rested.

I was trained early to survive systems that don't believe you. My first encounter wasn't academia – it was the United States healthcare system. At 19, newly diagnosed, I learned what it means to be simultaneously pathologised and disbelieved. I learned that care often came with conditions, that you had to appear stable to be treated as human. My 20s became a masterclass in masking: look competent, stay quiet and perform wellness convincingly enough to be left alone. I also learned how to make pain legible, even marketable. In academia, we're trained to turn hardship into merit – to package survival as resilience, to sell our struggle in the language of grants and fellowships. Academia loves a redemption arc. I have the Diversity, Equity and Inclusion (DEI) awards to prove it. Those lessons translated seamlessly into academic life.

Academia loves a polished survivor. The performance of resilience looks a lot like productivity, and I was good at both. I worked through illness, through pregnancies, through the endless bureaucratic churn of higher education. The university is a machine that runs on unpaid hours and emotional labour, and I fed it willingly. Writing grants at midnight, going days without sleep before paper deadlines, replying to panicked student emails at dawn, sitting through meetings that could have been a collective scream. I wrote some of this as a postdoc in a blog article titled 'My World Building: Story of a Disabled Academic', which drew a lot of attention from fellow tired academics (Ringland, 2020). Little did I know that was me in slow-motion crash and burn. Since becoming a professor, the work has never stopped expanding, and the budgets have never stopped shrinking. Administrative labour trickled down like runoff, pooling at the feet of faculty already ankle-deep in service.

I know I'm still one of the lucky ones. I have a full-time job, healthcare and relative stability. The adjuncts and graduate workers who keep the university running face this same exhaustion with none of the safety nets. It's hard not to feel both grateful and guilty – grateful to have survived thus far, guilty to know survival has become the metric.

Beyond the campus, the air itself feels hostile to thinking. We're living through a slow cultural drift towards anti-intellectualism, where expertise is suspect and attention is currency. The spaces that once connected us – social media, public forums, even university websites – have been hollowed out, optimised for outrage instead of understanding. The algorithms reward certainty, not curiosity. Nuance is bad for engagement. What was once public infrastructure for thinking together has become a marketplace for reaction, where ideas are stripped of parts and sold for clicks. And somehow, we're expected to keep producing knowledge in a culture that increasingly devalues it.

And through it all, our students are trying their best to hold it together. They're balancing debt, disability, jobs, caregiving and the constant noise of a world that feels uncertain. I see their effort in every late-night email, every office-hour conversation where they're doing their best to stay hopeful. They ask big, brave questions about the future – sometimes out loud, sometimes between the lines. The emotional work of holding space for all that complexity is real. I do it willingly because I remember what it feels like to want so much from a world that keeps shifting under your feet. But compassion doesn't come with a course release, and every small act of care adds another invisible line to the ledger of labour we rarely name – and certainly don't acknowledge on our personnel reviews.

None of it happens all at once. It's the slow suffocation of a profession by paperwork and precarity – the constant hum of being both indispensable and disposable. And yet, despite it all, we keep showing up. We teach. We mentor. We make spreadsheets for students' deadlines and bake cookies for lab meetings. We keep tending to the small fires of meaning wherever we can find them.

The institution may be decomposing, but the people inside it are still trying, stubbornly, to build something that feels like care.

For neurodivergent scholars, the institution's expectations map perfectly onto our vulnerabilities. Overcommitment is mistaken for passion, masking is mistaken for professionalism and hyperfocus is mistaken for productivity. We're praised for endurance until the moment we can't sustain it. Burnout doesn't just silence our work – it distorts how others see our competence and worth.

THE FIRE THAT FEEDS ITSELF

For neurodivergent academics, burnout isn't a personal shortcoming – it's an occupational hazard. The university depends on our overcommitment to survive. The more we give, the more it asks. And we do give, because care is part of how we understand our work.

Invisible labour has become our default mode. Many of us mentor the students who fall between the cracks – the ones who remind us of younger versions of ourselves. We offer the listening, the flexibility, the second chances the system won't. We design accessible materials, sit on equity committees and review policies that should have been equitable to begin with. None of it counts as 'real' work, but it's the glue that keeps our programs humane. It's also exhausting.

I say *we* here, but that 'we' deserves scrutiny. Not every neurodivergent academic experiences – or survives – this system in the same way. My version of 'we' tends to include those of us who have some measure of institutional security – people buffered, however slightly, by whiteness, citizenship, able-bodiedness, class or tenure-track proximity. Many of our colleagues and friends live without those protections, carrying heavier burdens of precarity, racism, ableism and structural exclusion. Some have already been pushed out or are holding on through sheer will and community care. When I write 'we', I mean the ones still inside the walls, exhausted but still trying to make space for others – though the real work of resistance stretches far beyond any one office, lab or job title. It's an incomplete *we*, a porous coalition held together by care and the hope that none of us are doing this alone.

I see this most clearly in my own research group, the Misfit Lab – a name my students lovingly chose for themselves, inspired by Rosemary Garland-Thomson's writing on misfitting (Garland-Thomson, 2011). The lab began as an experiment in refusal: what if a research group were designed around access and care rather than performance and output? We built it together, consciously and imperfectly, in crip time. When my students and I co-wrote a blog post called '*Creating a Lab with a Culture of Care*', we described it as an ongoing process (Eagle et al., 2022). Something is always being adjusted and we'll never be finished. We wrote about treating academic milestones as checkpoints rather than moral tests, about making space to discuss accessibility needs openly, about rest as a baseline, not a reward.

In that piece, my students articulated what I had been trying to build. A space where access is assumed, where people can disclose – or not disclose – without fear, and where care isn't a side project but the infrastructure of the work itself. They wrote that 'rest in our lab is not a reward that needs to be earned, but rather something to be taken whenever necessary'. I return to that line often, because it names something academia systematically unlearns from us: that care and productivity are not opposites.

And yet, even inside this small bubble of resistance, we're still tethered to the larger machinery of the university. Budgets, deadlines and institutional expectations seep in through every crack. The emotional labour that sustains a culture of care – checking in, holding space, negotiating flexibility – remains invisible in the metrics that define success. We are praised for compassion only when it doesn't interfere with efficiency.

Masking adds another layer. We hide sensory overwhelm, executive dysfunction, pain and panic because professionalism demands composure. We learn to make our neurodivergence legible only when it's palatable: 'creativity', 'innovation', 'different ways of thinking'. The rest we keep tucked out of sight. As Margaret Price writes in *Mad at School*, the academy's version of 'participation' assumes a single kind of mind and body – alert, consistent and unflinching (Price, 2011). To diverge from that template is to risk being read as unreliable.

For disabled and chronically ill scholars, that risk compounds. Alison Kafer's *Feminist, Queer, Crip* reminds us that institutions still frame disability as a problem to be accommodated, not a culture to be valued (Kafer, 2013). Many of us do our own accommodations on the fly: adjusting lighting, teaching through migraines and reshuffling deadlines around pain. We make accessibility possible for others even as we're denied it ourselves. And yet, this same system also offers something rare – flexibility. Academia's porous boundaries mean we can sometimes work from bed, shift our hours or design research that reflects our values. That freedom is part of what keeps many of us here. But it's a double-edged kind of freedom, one that allows us to survive within an institution that is still not built to sustain us.

And the burden isn't distributed evenly. Gender, race, caregiving, class and chronic illness – all intersect to make some of us more visible and more vulnerable. Women, especially women of colour and disabled women, are often expected to perform care as proof of belonging. It's not enough to do the job. We must also soften it for everyone else. The expectation of emotional labour follows us into every meeting and student interaction. The price of being 'approachable' is depletion.

This is the double exhaustion of neurodivergent life in the academy. We are both subjects of accommodation and its quiet architects. We spend our days building kinder systems inside institutions that mistake kindness for inefficiency. Burnout, in this context, is not failure – it's evidence. It shows us exactly what the system consumes to keep running.

LIVING INSIDE THE ASHES

Burnout doesn't always look like collapse. Sometimes it's invisible. For me, it's forgetting words mid-sentence, losing track of emails the second I read them, a body that seems permanently out of calibration. The migraines arrive like clockwork, light behind my eyes sharpening until even the hum of my monitor feels hostile. My joints ache from too many hours in front of a screen and too few spent outside. It's a body and mind running out of buffer, pretending to still have capacity.

Later, when I read Dr. Neff's description of autistic burnout in *Self-Care for Autistic People* (Neff, 2024) 'unrelenting fatigue, heightened sensory sensitivities, skills and functioning decline, emotional dysregulation, diminished tolerance for change, social isolation, and masking' –

I felt seen. For once, the patterns I'd been living weren't framed as personal failure but as something real, shared and nameable. That recognition was both relief and reckoning, and it's one of the reasons I'm writing this essay. I hope someone else might read these words and feel a little less alone.

At some point, I stopped waiting to 'recover' and started learning how to live inside it. The exhaustion never really leaves, just finds a rhythm. There are good weeks, and there are weeks when opening an email feels like lifting a boulder. I try not to measure myself against the version of me who could once do more. These days, 'good enough' has become its own quiet victory. Sometimes surviving the term *is* the publication.

Recovery – if you can call it that – isn't a return to normalcy. It's a refusal to keep performing it. It's saying no before collapse, delegating without guilt and letting unread messages sit there like small acts of rebellion. It's learning to rest without permission. As a neurodivergent person, I've realised that rest doesn't always look restful. Sometimes it's reorganising my notes, sometimes it's gaming, sometimes it's sitting in silence after class letting the day drain out of my body. My wellness plan, if I'm honest, is about 30% rebellion, 40% naps and 30% caffeine.

What sustains me isn't institutional wellness programmes or productivity hacks – it's people. Colleagues who remind me that 'you don't owe anyone this'. Students whose curiosity briefly cuts through the fog. Friends who text memes and playful GIFs upon request. These care webs don't fix the system, but they make it survivable. Care, in this sense, isn't just kindness – it's strategy.

Burnout has stripped away the illusion of control, but it's also taught me how to listen: to my body, my limits, my students and the quiet in-between moments when the work actually matters.

Burnout isn't wisdom, exactly, but it's a kind of embodied knowledge – a record of what happens when human beings are stretched too thin in institutions built for endless output. What remains, if we're lucky, is clarity. I don't believe in balance anymore. I believe in seasons. Some days I write. Some days I rest. Most days I just keep the fire from going out.

MANIFESTO FOR THE BURNED OUT

We deserve to be more than our output.

We deserve rest that isn't conditional, rest that isn't earned by collapse.

We deserve to work in systems that value care as scholarship, not side work.

We deserve meetings that end early, budgets that include access and policies written with disabled and neurodivergent people at the table from the start.

We deserve to say no without fear that it will close a door.

We deserve colleagues who see boundaries as respect, not resistance.

We deserve mentorship that doesn't reproduce harm, and leadership that knows exhaustion is not excellence.

We deserve to bring our full selves – disabled, neurodivergent, complicated, human – into our classrooms and labs without apology.

We deserve to study, teach and imagine futures where thriving isn't the exception.

Burnout taught me that survival is not the goal. The goal is transformation. The university will not save us, but we might save each other – through small acts of care, quiet refusals and honest conversations that make space for truth. The work ahead is not to rebuild the same system but to build something gentler in its place.

EMBER THAT STILL GLOWS

The emails still arrive. They always will. The inbox has become its own kind of weather – shifting, relentless, occasionally beautiful in its patterns. I no longer measure myself by how quickly I can clear it. Some messages wait longer now. Some will never be answered. The world doesn't end.

I'm still tired. Not the poetic kind of tired that signals transformation, just the real, bone-deep kind that comes from years of caring more than the system ever could. I'm still in it. The difference is that I know what matters now. I've learned where my limited energy belongs and what can fall away. My priorities look different than they used to – different, too, from what might make sense for anyone else. Every academic I know is fighting their own version of this exhaustion, shaping a life around what they refuse to lose. For me, that means protecting time for my students, for my family, for the quiet work that still feels meaningful. It's not balance. It's choosing, again and again, not to let the wrong things win.

There are still nights when I get it wrong. When I stay up too late answering emails I could have ignored or agree to something I know will cost more energy than I have. The glow from my screen still pulls me in, the way fire does when you're too close to it. But I'm learning to let that be okay. Some seasons still ask too much. Some sparks still catch. What's changed is that I can see it happening now. I can step back before I burn. And when I can't, there are people – students, colleagues, friends – who remind me to rest, to eat, to close the laptop. Community doesn't extinguish the fire, but it makes it survivable.

I used to think the goal was balance, to find the perfect ratio of rest to productivity. Now I know that balance is a myth built for people who have never had to choose between the two. What I have instead is rhythm: seasons of motion and stillness, sparks and embers. There are days when I can write whole paragraphs, and others when I close my laptop mid-sentence and walk away. Both count.

Burnout taught me to listen – to my body, my limits and to the silences between demands. It taught me that honesty is its own kind of care and that survival, in this place, is not a small thing.

REFERENCES

Eagle, T., Baltaxe-Admony, L. B., & Ringland, K. (2022, May 10). *Creating a lab with a culture of care*. Medium. https://medium.com/misfitlabs/creating-a-lab-with-a-culture-of-care-2b19bb0b2a22

Garland-Thomson, R. (2011). Misfits: A feminist materialist disability concept. *Hypatia*, *26*(3), 591–609.

Kafer, A. (2013). *Feminist, queer, crip*. Indiana University Press.

Neff, M. A. (2024). *Self-care for autistic people: 100+ ways to recharge, de-Stress, and unmask*. Adams Media Corporation.

Price, M. (2011). *Mad at school: Rhetorics of mental disability and academic life*. University of Michigan Press.

Ringland, K. (2020, August 21). *My world building: Story of a disabled academic*. Medium. https://kateringland.medium.com/my-world-building-story-of-a-disabled-academic-cc9633560494

7

BECOMING A SENSITIVE SCHOLAR: NAVIGATING THE ACADEMIC ASSEMBLAGES IN EAST ASIA

MARIO LIONG

National Taipei University, Taiwan

ABSTRACT

This chapter traces the unintended journey of a highly sensitive academic navigating institutional assemblages across East Asia and beyond. Exhaustion in striving to fulfil set goals was previously understood as a personal deficit until the author encountered the knowledge of sensory processing sensitivity (SPS). Drawing on Deleuze and Guattari, the author reframes SPS as a 'diagrammatic operator' that modulates capacity in various academic assemblages. High sensitivity amplified heavy teaching loads, evaluation regimes and time-limited work security, creating anxiety and making self-care difficult. Yet close teacher-student interactions, collegial support, research-oriented temporal space and stable living and work environments enabled sensitivity to promote joy and insights. Instead of exhorting individual resilience, this chapter argues for recomposing academic assemblages to embrace neurodivergence: Institutional spaces for negotiated goals, collegial support and temporal room for creativity can sustain productivity and well-being better than performance-driven metrics.

Keywords: Sensory processing sensitivity (SPS); academic assemblages; sensory environment; East Asian neurodivergent academics; Deleuze and Guattari

Source: Artwork by Melissa Vallence.
A Portrait of Mario Liong.

INTRODUCTION

More than 200 students sat in tiers above me in a lecture hall at a college in Hong Kong. To me, their faces dissolved into a single surface, yet they were alive with whispers that grew into a low, disturbing roar within me. I paused, and the room became quiet. I resumed, and the side talk returned; I felt my words like pebbles tossed into a fast river. With a deep breath, I called the class to order, and it worked for a few minutes; yet the current of side talk always regained force. My energy depleted, and my passion for lecturing slowly drifted away. When I shared this with my colleagues and sought their advice, they shrugged and said, 'That happens to everyone—just speak louder to cover their voices'. For them, it was a nuisance, but for me, it was a sonic storm that constantly robbed my attention and energy, leaving my body humming with fatigue and anxiety about not being able to stay in control.

Years later, I learnt about high sensory sensitivity – a physiological trait characterised by greater awareness of environmental subtleties, deeper information processing and pronounced emotional responsiveness to stimuli (Aron & Aron, 1997; Rock, 2022). With the help of the Highly Sensitive Person (HSP) scale (Aron & Aron, 1997) and the consultation of a psychotherapist, I realised that high sensory sensitivity impacted me in many ways, personally and professionally. This knowledge transformed my understanding of that lecture-hall experience; it was no longer a personal failing but an assemblage,[1] as Deleuze and Guattari (1987) described, of acoustics, space, student norms, time pressures, institutional rules and my own sensory thresholds.

In this chapter, I adopt that perspective, drawing on Deleuze and Guattari's concepts to make sense of my life as a highly sensitive academic working across various countries, particularly in East Asia. I reflect on how sensory sensitivity, together with other entities, has shaped my academic journey and my ways of coping – for better or for worse. Although I write in the first person, I am aware that I am not the only agent. I am a body among spaces,

---

[1]Assemblage is a concrete set-up of heterogeneous elements (including people, space, objects, rules or concepts, among others) that work together for a time.

rules, norms, intensities and other bodies – an ever-shifting set of couplings that both constrain and enable what I can do.

The following sections trace my academic journey, followed by my discovery of high sensory sensitivity and its meaning. I then discuss how Deleuze and Guattari's concepts can help interpret my experiences as a highly sensitive academic, and finally, I conclude with the coping mechanisms I have learned.

TRAILING AND STRUGGLING INTO THE UNINTENDED LAND

As an undergraduate in psychology, I did not intend to become an academic but imagined myself as a psychotherapist. I enjoyed listening to people's stories (and still do) and helping them adopt new perspectives to resolve their issues. However, my less-than-top-notch academic performance prevented me from entering the profession. Feeling uncertain about my future, a friend's enthusiastic persuasion nudged me towards a research master's in gender studies. The pleasure of learning theories – the sense of a stubborn intellectual knot slowly loosening – kept me moving through this unintended territory.

My PhD studies in anthropology in Hong Kong allowed me to learn qualitative methods and practise building concepts from lived experiences. I studied fatherhood as a site where masculinity both breaks and remakes itself within the family. This research[2] led me to conduct fieldwork in several men's centres and interviews with middle-aged men who shared their hardships and dreams with me. I was surprised and deeply grateful that they shared something deep

[2]A comprehensive account of the research is available in the following monograph: Liong, M. (2017). *Chinese fatherhood, gender and family: Father mission*. London: Palgrave Macmillan.

with a young stranger like me. The fieldwork[3] lasted a year and a half, and its completion marked the beginning of my first full-time teaching position.

Driven by a passion to share knowledge and inspire students to learn independently, I joined a two-year college while finishing my dissertation. The teaching load was heavy: up to six different courses and 16 contact hours a week. The episode described at the beginning of this chapter occurred during this period. Although large lectures were difficult to manage, smaller tutorials encouraged close student–teacher relationships, which make teaching and mentoring enjoyable. However, my days were consumed by preparation and consultation. I worked in a shared office on one campus, where thin soundproofing between offices allowed small talk and consultation discussions to leak into my workspace, and in shared cubicle workstations on another campus, where colleagues talked and moved around. Consultations could be interrupted, and attention during preparation could be cut short. Students also walked in without appointments to ask questions or negotiate grades, dissolving the boundary between preparation and consultation. Although listening to light music with earphones helped maintain some degree of working territory, chronic sleep deprivation and heavy teaching loads made reading in such an environment challenging, especially after lunch. The assemblage consumed not only time but also the intellectual capacity.

The management's insistence on an English-only policy in lecturing created barriers in the learning process for many students. When students could not follow the class content, pressure emerged for the instructor to either switch to Cantonese (the local language) and face management warnings, or spend extra consultation time after class explaining the same materials in Cantonese. In addition, the heavy teaching load and back-to-back tight class

---

[3]For readers interested in a fuller discussion, the fieldwork experiences are accounted for in two published articles that examine how my masculinities and positionality shaped the research process: Liong, M. (2015). Like father, like son: negotiation of masculinity in the ethnographic context in Hong Kong. *Gender, Place & Culture*, 22(7), 937–953; and Liong, M. (2015). In the shadow of deception: Ethical dilemma, positionality, and reflexivity in ethnographic fieldwork. *Qualitative Research Journal*, *15*(1), 61–73.

schedule placed constant time anxiety in my chest about running late for the next class and failing to cover all designated materials. This was when my sensitivity – although I did not yet recognise it then – manifested as a narrowing of capacity. I had difficulty refusing students' requests as I absorbed their sense of urgency and carried the anxiety privately, as if I were completely responsible for solving the issue. The management took teaching evaluations seriously, and appraisals held every two years required detailed descriptions of teaching and administrative contributions, further pushing me to work harder. After a full day, my mind often went blank, and my capacity to speak was completely depleted. On some busy days, I could barely remember which class I was about to teach, let alone find time to write my dissertation and develop my research. I walked quickly everywhere, trying to reclaim time in the dense, fast-paced city. During this period, headaches and stomach problems crept in, though I did not realise they were caused by lack of sleep. I continued pushing myself to do more.

After completing my PhD, I began seriously seeking a position with better research opportunities. A postdoctoral position in Sweden came after numerous applications. The experience flipped everything – geographically and academically. There was no teaching requirement, and I could devote my time entirely to writing. This period deterritorialised[4] my academic trajectory in Hong Kong as I learned to write publishable papers, write grant proposals and present my research to international scholars. With no external pressure, I finally had time and space to heal my body through adequate rest and by appreciating tranquillity and nature. However, the pressure shifted inward: I viewed the two-year position as a limited window to write, setting myself a goal of producing one manuscript per month. I managed to generate manuscripts and drafts that later became publications and proposals, yet the anxiety of not doing enough never subsided.

[4]Deleuze and Guattari used the term deterritorialisation to mean a shift from an established stability. It is a force that loosens or breaks a pattern. It may open up new possibilities and take away the support that holds things together (Colebrook, 2020; Deleuze & Guattari, 1987).

LOOKING FOR A POSITION TO SETTLE AND DEVELOP

Six months after returning to Hong Kong, I joined a four-year teaching college. It was an improvement on my first position, offering small internal research funds, support for applying for major grants, smaller class sizes and two to three courses per semester – even though contact hours remained high. There was no longer the disruptive classroom noise from side conversations, and that change mattered. I could finally turn the manuscripts I had drafted earlier into publications and begin to imagine a path back to a research university. After several applications, an offer from a university in Japan ignited hope for a more stable research environment.

Arriving in Japan, everything felt bright and new. I had never lived there and had seldom even travelled there. The language was a wall I decided to climb slowly. I was hopeful that I could manage it after a few years of private lessons. Teaching five courses per semester meant heavy preparation, even if the contact hours were half those in Hong Kong. The international environment of the programme I taught in made me feel at home. It was particularly soothing as a foreigner arriving in a country where I knew no one and did not speak the language. The students were attentive, friendly and respectful towards teachers, and I was able to befriend some international students and colleagues and spend time with them occasionally.

After the first year, I had settled in and begun to move my research forward, albeit slowly. However, without the ability to speak Japanese, qualitative research was unrealistic. Qualitative work has been the most satisfying part of scholarship: it allows for deep immersion into people's lived experiences to extract meaningful concepts from the textures and contradictions of their accounts. When transcripts, concepts and analysis come together and compose something meaningful, this assemblage not only produces joy but also expands my capacity to think and write. In addition, the time limit of my fixed-term contract ticked audibly in the background, evoking a familiar sense of uncertainty I had felt in Sweden. I therefore shifted temporarily to conducting a quantitative study while devoting time each day to learn the language, believing that fluency might help me secure a permanent post. The day-to-day assemblage – teaching, administrative work, collegial interactions and everyday language demands – was smooth, yet my research line of flight[5] was constrained by advanced language requirements and limited time. Just before the outbreak of COVID-19, I noticed job openings in Taiwan and decided to give them a try. I eventually found a vacancy for a scholar in the sociology of gender and received an offer for my current position following an interview.

I arrived in Taiwan during COVID, relieved to be somewhere with no lockdown and few infections. The first sight of the campus – broad lawns behind the gate and a pond with fish and ducks – left an impression of spaciousness. This first impression was later confirmed by a lighter teaching load and research support, with fewer performance pressures. The new environment allowed more room to explore topics and frameworks, experiment with teaching methods and grow personally. I even revisited my study of psychology – initially for teaching purposes, but later as a research and personal interest in high sensory sensitivity. The 'spaciousness' is also manifested in mentoring student research assistants. Many students at this university possess excellent research skills and serve as capable research assistants. Having them on my research team can be deeply joyful when I notice that they are serious about acquiring skills in interviewing, reading literature and conducting analysis, demonstrating care, responsibility, precision and intellectual curiosity. However, it can be troubling when these tasks are treated as extra assignments and burdens, and when agreed-upon timelines slip without communication. In particular, I feel disappointed when my openness in wanting to know what has happened and my support for them to complete the work were evaded. After all, with no contract clock ticking in the background, the assemblage – light teaching, ample research time, institutional support and collaborative colleagues – has made it possible to explore minoritarian topics and write with care.

[5]The concept of line of flight, introduced by Deleuze and Guattari (1987), refers to the path of transformation within an assemblage. It is the process of deterritorialisation, through which an existing set-up undergoes change and forms connections with new arrangements.

DISCOVERING HIGH SENSORY SENSITIVITY

While I had regained an interest in psychology through teaching an introductory course, a friend disclosed to me that she was a highly sensitive person and encouraged me to read about it. As I began to research, I was struck by the high visibility of HSP in Japan and Taiwan. In Japan, HSP books, both translated and locally written, are abundant; in contrast, in Taiwan, the majority of HSP books are translations from abroad, including some from Japan. However, popular print and online magazines in Taiwan feature a collection of easily accessible pieces about HSP, aiming to introduce high sensory sensitivity to their readers and to offer them a vocabulary for self-discovery, affirming their qualities and resisting the common devaluation of being 'too sensitive'. I sensed that young people in Taiwan demonstrate a generational ease with psychotherapy and a broader view of mental health as an ordinary part of self-care. Although high sensory sensitivity is not yet widely recognised in Taiwan, some young people are aware of it and even incorporate the label into their self-introductions. This cultural climate reorganised my own self-discovery journey by incorporating my sensitivity into my personal growth and academic pursuit, rather than treating it as a flaw that needed to be hidden.

Sensory processing sensitivity (SPS) was first studied by Aron and Aron (1997), who distinguished SPS from introversion or generalised emotionality and established it as a distinct dimension of human neuro-variability with measurable psychological and physiological markers. Beyond greater awareness of sensory input, individuals high in SPS tend to engage in deeper cognitive reflection, stronger emotional reactivity and more intense sensory processing (Aron et al., 2012). Highly sensitive people (HSPs), on one hand, are empathetic, self-reflective and conscientious; we are easily and deeply moved by art, music and interpersonal experiences. On the other hand, we are susceptible to feeling overwhelmed under pressure or stress and when exposed to competing demands (Acevedo et al., 2021). We require more downtime and rest to recover, during which deep cognitive processing and memory consolidation occur more vigorously than in non-HSPs (Acevedo et al., 2021). HSPs are also influenced by their environments. We thrive more than others in positive, supportive and accepting environments (Pluess & Belsky, 2013). Conversely, environments characterised by high stress, low support, disorganisation or work overload can lead to greater fatigue, anxiety, depression and reduced physical health (Jagiellowicz et al., 2020).

Few studies have focused on HSPs in the education profession, particularly in tertiary education and research. However, two dissertations on highly sensitive teachers shed light on how SPS influences educators. Lindsay (2017) found that teachers with strong sensitivity traits reported higher engagement when given sufficient preparation time and access to quiet environments before instruction begins because their deep processing, empathy, emotional reactivity for supporting students and sensitivity to others' moods and gestures made them vulnerable to overstimulation and fatigue. Tillmann (2019) added that highly sensitive teachers struggled to maintain work–life balance, often feeling insecure about how much extra time and effort to invest in their teaching and mentoring, especially when feedback was limited, and expectations were high.

From these findings, it is easy to imagine how harsh academic life can be for HSPs striving to achieve work–life balance and manage stress. The highly competitive environment of constant evaluations, appraisals and performance metrics generates immense pressure and self-doubt, particularly when feedback and support are limited. We may overwork ourselves to meet expectations, leading to fatigue or even burnout. Ultimately, we flourish more than others in positive, supportive environments but can deteriorate rapidly in negative ones (Jagiellowicz et al., 2020; Pluess & Belsky, 2013).

WHERE DELEUZE AND GUATTARI 'CLICKED': SENSITIVITY AS A DIAGRAM, NOT A DIAGNOSIS

Learning the above gradually revealed that SPS and the knowledge of it are, following Deleuze and Guattari's (1987) conception, diagrammatic operators within the different assemblages I inhabited. A diagrammatic operator functions like a portable switch that reorganises how elements interact without being bound to any fixed configuration. It reroutes the entities and intensities within an assemblage that remains open to transformation. Viewed in this way, SPS is not a fragile essence; rather, it modulates thresholds and redirects flows of attention and affect. In compositions that cohere, it increases my capacity to act – enhancing concentration, insight and connection; in difficult compositions, it constrains capacity – producing sadness, fatigue, or shutdown. The question thus shifts from what SPS is to what it enables or disables within a given arrangement – and how that arrangement might be redesigned to expand capacity.

In this sense, my academic journey in Hong Kong was overcoded with metrics; Sweden opened a smooth space but introduced a self-made structure; Japan stabilised the work environment while narrowing research; Taiwan offered balance. My sensitivity made these differences intelligible: some capacities were enabled while others were diminished. In what follows, I highlight certain moments in my academic journey to illustrate this perspective.

The colleges where I worked in Hong Kong quantified teaching through metrics and comparative scores. Management treated these scores seriously: not only were they reviewed during appraisals, but teachers who scored below the threshold were also questioned each semester. Although the policy aimed to make teachers accountable, my resistance to this overcoding metrics apparatus provoked ambivalence and performance anxiety intensified by SPS. Instead of yielding to indicator-optimisation strategies, such as grade inflation for better evaluations or prioritising entertainment in the class over serious learning, my response involved transparent rubrics, rigorous feedback, democratic discussions in grade adjustments, and class designs that fostered learning. Nevertheless, students' desire to have high scores for further study and emphasis on educational qualifications over knowledge acquisition encouraged competition for ever-higher scores during discussions and adjustments. My small attempt to resist score management and my empathy about students' academic struggles were recaptured as grade bargaining, rather than a space for learning. The awakening came when a student slammed a chair after a discussion did not go his way. I learned that empathy is not always a virtue. It can be captured in some assemblages. This assemblage – school system, educational norms, students' aspirations, my resistance and my SPS – captured and translated empathy into anxiety, frustration, disappointment and hurt in me. In the next semester, I withdrew the negotiation element and reinforced boundaries through detailed written feedback justifying the grades.

Applying Deleuze and Guattari's ideas to the anecdote at the beginning of the chapter, in relation to my SPS, releases me from the perception of being opposed to the students and from subsequent self-blame. A management apparatus fixated on cost efficiency organised large classes with dense seating, loose participation norms and tight schedules – all of which amplified conversational noise. Although I can now recognise this as a compositional misfit through the Deleuze and Guattari lens, at the time my SPS thresholds registered the noise as 'disrespectful disturbance'. A strong affect of self-doubt, helplessness and shame set in. Calling it out offered only brief relief, and repetition drained my energy. Moreover, performance anxiety, as a result of the amplified stress in meeting the institutional performance appraisal and self-demand by SPS, co-composed the scene, bringing forth overthinking classroom management strategies, repeatedly rehearsing variations of the teaching material to maintain attention, and physiological unrest the night before teaching. Nevertheless, that traumatic semester taught me to appreciate a large, attentive audience.

The Swedish postdoctoral position deterritorialised the earlier heavy teaching tempo and offered a research assemblage that generated elation: no teaching, a quiet office, autonomous schedules, colleagues who read drafts for one another, and a small reading group. Elation in research arises from solving analytical challenges, acquiring skills or finally understanding and applying complex concepts. It is not a mere personal mood but an increase in the capacity to act, or joy in Deleuzian terms (Deleuze, 1990). My SPS does not produce elation by itself but modulates or amplifies the intensities within the assemblage. When the set-up is facilitative, SPS augments coherence and produces surges of concentration, inspiration, synthesis and connection. However, this research assemblage had a two-year limit, overcoding the process with anxiety, as SPS tuned the elation into a desire for productivity.

Therefore, in the Swedish research environment, research capacity rose – I produced a series of drafts that later became published articles and research proposals; yet the presence of the contract clock kept the sense of urgency alive, generating a persistent internal reminder that I was still not doing enough.

Japan reterritorialised my academic journey in a more stabilising way. The international environment of friendly colleagues and respectful students and a predictable routine of repeated teaching blocks, allowed my nervous system to unwind. SPS sparked joy in such a teaching environment, reigniting my enthusiasm for teaching and exploring innovative pedagogical approaches. In Deleuze and Guattari (1987)'s analogy, this assemblage composed refrains – repeated expressive patterns that create a calm and stable territory that is liveable. Yet that stabilisation came with a narrowing of research with the presence of advanced language requirements and contract time. COVID-19 further tightened the assemblage by restricting mobility and in-person encounters. In sum, the assemblage in Japan was composed of a smoother and calmer daily life that soothed my heightened sensitivity and enabled joy, but also of a more restrictive horizon for research work.

Taiwan recomposed the academic assemblage: attentive students, a manageable teaching load and administrative workload, capable research assistants, academically and emotionally supportive colleagues, language proficiency, job security and stability, and generous research funding. This assemblage facilitated exploratory research topics, and my SPS enhanced elation and increased research capacity – not in terms of quantity, as in the previous trajectory, but in terms of novelty and insight. In this context, SPS became an asset because it enables deeper sensitivity to hidden meanings and connections during data collection and analysis. Yet such gain is not guaranteed; it emerges only when the assemblage is supported by enabling scaffolding.

CONCLUSION: BECOMING SENSORIAL

SPS is often framed as something to be managed in the popular discourse. With Deleuze and Guattari's ideas, I now treat it as a switch that modulates my insight, motivation, emotional reactions and connections. It enables me to pursue overlooked research topics, discover insights and hidden messages during interviews, and connect with students who are eager to learn – when the assemblage is well composed. Nevertheless, my actions also play a role in shaping such assemblages: allowing sufficient time for completing projects, scheduling rest periods and creating conditions for calm and renewal. In hindsight, this revelation was made possible by my journey across different academic contexts. It is an ongoing experimental path of *becoming sensorial* – discovering stabilising patterns, accepting and allowing the need for space and time and allowing empathy to connect without being captured.

Sensitivity is not a weakness to hide or control but an integral part of the academic assemblage. In outcome-oriented work cultures that emphasise quantifiable productivity, simply preaching 'awareness of neurodivergence' is insufficient to prevent institutional overcoding that reduces every task to numbers. Instead, it is necessary to recompose local assemblages so that more bodies can act. Sensitive and other neurodivergent scholars co-compose the broader academic assemblage alongside all others. We can create space for rigorous work through well-tuned compositions. Then, emotion and rigour will cease to be seen as opposites, and cognitive diversity will move from utopia to practice.

REFERENCES

Acevedo, B. P., Santander, T., Marhenke, R., Aron, A., & Aron, E. (2021). Sensory processing sensitivity predicts individual differences in resting-state functional connectivity associated with depth of processing. *Neuropsychobiology*, *80*(2), 185–200.

Aron, E. N., & Aron, A. (1997). Sensory-processing sensitivity and its relation to introversion and emotionality. *Journal of personality and social psychology*, *73*(2), 345–368.

Aron, E. N., Aron, A., & Jagiellowicz, J. (2012). Sensory processing sensitivity: A review in the light of the evolution of biological responsivity. *Personality and Social Psychology Review*, *16*(3), 262–282.

Colebrook, C. (2020). *Understanding Deleuze*. Routledge.

Deleuze, G. (1990). *Expressionism and philosophy: Spinoza*. Zone Books.

Deleuze, G., & Guattari, F. (1987). *A thousand plateaus: Capitalism and schizophrenia* (Translation and Foreword by B. Massumi). University of Minnesota Press.

Jagiellowicz, J., Zarinafsar, S., & Acevedo, B. P. (2020). Health and social outcomes in highly sensitive persons. In B. P. Acevedo (Ed.), *The highly sensitive brain* (pp. 75–107). Academic Press.

Lindsay, J. S. (2017). *The highly sensitive teacher: Sensory-processing sensitivity, burnout, and self-efficacy in urban public school teachers* [Doctoral dissertation, University of California, Los Angeles]. ProQuest Dissertations & Theses Global.

Pluess, M., & Belsky, J. (2013). Vantage sensitivity: Individual differences in response to positive experiences. *Psychological Bulletin*, *139*(4), 901–916.

Rock, S. (2022). *Experiences of transformation in highly sensitive people: A narrative hermeneutical analysis through the lens of gender diversity* [Doctoral dissertation, California Institute of Integral Studies]. ProQuest Dissertations & Theses Global.

Tillmann, T. (2019). *Sensory-processing sensitivity in the context of the teaching profession and its demands: Blessing, curse or both?* [Doctoral dissertation, Ludwig-Maximilians-Universität München].

8

COMMANDER KEEN? PLAYING THE ACADEMIC GAME OF ENTHUSIASTIC INNOVATION CONSTRAINED BY INSTITUTIONAL HIERARCHIES

MATTHEW HARRISON

The University of Melbourne, Australia

ABSTRACT

This chapter reflects on the experiences of Associate Professor Matthew Harrison, a neurodivergent teacher-researcher navigating the often contradictory and emotionally charged terrain of academic life. Using the early 1990s Commander Keen game series as an organising metaphor, he maps the 'levels' of his journey from childhood to mid-career, illustrating how curiosity, justice sensitivity and unconventional thinking have shaped both his opportunities and challenges within institutions that frequently reward conformity.

This chapter explores the shift from early-career safety to the more politicised world of middle leadership, where visibility invites scrutiny, enthusiasm can be misread as ambition and masking becomes a form of professional armour. These reflections highlight the tension between wanting to contribute meaningfully to change and needing to survive systems not designed for people who think, feel, or communicate differently.

Alongside these pressures, Matt describes the profound importance of neurodivergent-led spaces, including community-centred gaming programmes and large-scale neurodiversity initiatives, which have allowed more authentic, values-aligned work and collaboration without the need for dilution of constant self-translation. These spaces function as the 'hidden levels' of the academic game, sustaining the author as they repeatedly re-enter more traditional university environments.

Keywords: Neurodivergent leadership; middle-career academics; academic identity; imposter syndrome; masking; mentors and mentees

INTRODUCTION

As a neurodivergent teacher-researcher, I argue that many of us bring ideas that challenge prevailing assumptions, whether by imagining new research directions, rethinking institutional systems or noticing possibilities in the so-called market that others overlook. While innovation is often linked to neurodivergence, this association is contested, particularly given critiques of 'superpower' narratives that obscure the material challenges experienced by neurominorities (Acevedo & Stolz, 2024). As a researcher working in the neurodiversity paradigm, my own tendency to see things differently has led to both meaningful successes and unintended discomfort for myself and, occasionally, others. Although some neurodivergent academics feel professionally unsafe to share their ideas due to experiences of marginalisation, this has not been my experience. Instead, I reflect here on the transition from a protected early-career environment into the more precarious and often frustrating space of mid-career leadership.

Source: Artwork by Melissa Vallence.
A Portrait of Matthew Harrison.

The broader neurodiversity movement itself arises from tensions related to cultural homogenisation and othering (Botha et al., 2024; Dwyer, 2022). Dynamics that are echoed in the experience of becoming a 'middle leader': where responsibility for others' decisions, the need to 'play a straight bat', and discomforting acts of diplomacy become routine. Moving further from the safety of my early mentor's guidance has sharpened my awareness of how their safety enabled creativity and authenticity, and has reinforced my need for spaces where hierarchy matters less than collaboration and shared values. Although I am not autistic, the themes identified by Hayward and Flower (2025) resonate strongly with my experiences of navigating relationships, bridging miscommunications, understanding my executive functioning, adjusting for sensory needs and relying on the kindness of others as I continue to find my way through academia.

With this prologue complete, this brings us to my selection of the title for this chapter. As someone who researches experiences of neurodivergence, education and gaming, I am a complete nerd. I have always been this way. I have a particular affinity for 1990s shareware titles, including ID software's seminal 2D platform game Command Keen: Invasion of the Vorticons; complete with pogo sticks, hidden areas and signs written in a hidden language that was catnip for neurodivergent gamers like myself. Also appealing was the choice afforded the player in largely playing the levels in an order that worked for them.

Naming this chapter after Commander Keen reflects both how I suspect my senior neurotypical colleagues perceive my boundless, if sometimes boundary-less, enthusiasm for change and how this chapter itself is structured, moving through stages of my career in an order that makes sense to me (and, hopefully, to you). It, of course, also provides licence to introduce metaphors related to a piece of software that is close to my heart. As a final note before launching into this chapter, most games have heroes, neutral non-playable characters, antagonists and flat-out monsters. I have taken inspiration from the wonderful Professor Sandra Thom-Jones and named those who were heroes in my story, but anonymised those who could be considered the antagonists. While apparently common in academia, I am very fortunate that I have yet to encounter a true monster.

LEVEL 1: EXPLOITING THE GLITCHES IN THE GAME AS A CHILD WITH A LOUD VOICE

I was never a quiet student (nor a quiet adult), and I would often want to go off the conventional path, looking for other (better) ways to do things. Of course, this annoyed some people. Even as a child, I had an irrepressible instinct to share my thoughts, whether I was invited to or not. In particular, my nature at my rather conservative high school was to speak up and to try to bend the rules. Guided by a strong sense of justice inherited from my parents, I believed that if people better understood a situation and I showed them 'the better way', positive change would follow. I now recognise that feeling safe enough to speak up and to test limits was itself a position of privilege.

This voicing of concern caused both tension and change, sometimes simultaneously. My most audacious effort at politicking was lobbying for inline hockey as a school sport. Half the teachers rolled their eyes, declaring it an 'anti-social fringe sport', while the other half ranged from being mildly bemused to genuinely thrilled by the productive chaos. Having allies with both the power and the will to support change was critical, but being vocal also meant making enemies. A calculated risk I knowingly took.

But, after sharing this anecdote, it is important to share that I wasn't loud all the time. During my Year 12, the build-up to the second Iraq War was palpable, with friends parroting their parents' more conservative takes. I knew in my gut it was wrong, and I wanted to stand up against it, but I was also painfully aware of how fragile my social world was. At 18, the risk of losing friends felt scarier than global conflict. So, I kept my head down, biting my tongue when I wanted to express frustration. That silence was its own kind of lesson. I look back with some guilt that I didn't speak more loudly about my values, but I also recognise with self-compassion that I was young.

Year 12 was also a bit of a revelation for me in terms of understanding my brain. I had stumbled through Year 11, failing my midyear Physics exam and scraping by in Maths and Science; subjects that I had dutifully enrolled in because that was what the 'clever kids' were meant to do if they wanted a good university entrance ranking. The truth was, I found them frustrating and dull. The only spark that year came from my two humanities subjects, Literature and History, which I not only passed but also genuinely enjoyed. This huge change in my academic performance was a result of accidently figuring out my neurodivergent brain (without having that language or any diagnostic label) with help from Mrs.

O'Shea, my Year 11 History teacher (and then my Year 12 Literature teacher), and completely changing what I was studying to an eclectic mishmash of subjects that actually interested me. Funnily enough, I could actually do academics well when I followed my strengths and interests (Kpolvie et al., 2014).

Level 1 final boss battle: facing the tension between values and not being socially isolated.

Level 1 academic life lesson power up: speaking up matters, but it is also important to be strategic in how the message is delivered to avoid being labelled as obnoxious.

LEVEL 2: CHOOSING THE WRONG LEVEL BEFORE FINDING THE RIGHT ONE

When I look back at my first year of university, I can only describe it as an academic regression of spectacular proportions. My first-year results did not make my parents proud. After one year, I dropped out, travelled for a while and eventually stumbled my way back into study through a Bachelor of Arts (International Studies). But I discovered a 'hidden level' in this course: a placement I found myself in Ho Chi Minh City in Vietnam. This changed everything. I had convinced the course coordinator to allow me to do an internship at a school for children living on the street, with the school being funded by the Australian Department of Foreign Affairs and Trade. My brief was to be safely tucked away in administration, developing a fund-raising plan and organising a charity soccer (football) tournament for local donors. Due to staffing shortages, I soon found myself instead standing in front of a class, colourful pens and glue stick in hand, and feeling in my element. Teaching, it turned out, was a good fit for me and my brain. It was messy and unpredictable and deeply human, and it made me feel like I was doing something meaningful.

So I decided to select a 'different level'. I returned to study, this time for teacher education, and before long I had planted my feet on the slippery slope of teacher life. As someone who struggles to do only one thing at a time (surprise narrative twist: ADHD), a Master of Education and PhD came next. My research was and continues to be around supporting social inclusion for children and young adults with disabilities/neurodivergence through video game-based programs. Around the time I started my PhD, my supervisor asked me to cover one of his coding classes, which quickly ballooned into a precarious but exciting string of opportunities. I knew I probably only had 'one life' in this academic game, so I had to avoid taking hits and just survive for as long as possible. I said yes to everything, just grateful that someone thought I still belonged in the room. For someone whose parents were both teachers, education had always been framed as important, with The University of Melbourne being positioned as the pinnacle of Australian education; something that seemed far-fetched to me. Yet here I was, working within the then named Melbourne Graduate School of Education, insecurely clutching at contracts and hoping no one would notice that I still felt like an imposter. I was very much just happy to be here.

> *Level 2 final boss battle:* trying to be all things to all people to maintain precarious employment.
>
> *Level 2 life lesson power up:* to not be afraid to say something isn't a good fit and do the things that make you want to get out of bed in the morning as much as possible (but most people also have bills to pay).

LEVEL 3: BEING HANDED THE CONTROLLER FOR A SUSTAINABLE ACADEMIC CAREER

I was first invited into the fold by my former PhD supervisor, who led the Information Communication Technology (ICT) team. At the time, I was invited to co-teach a Master of Education class on entry-level coding and game-making. I was, quite frankly, chuffed to be asked. While I had never thought of myself as an 'academic', I did have a background as a self-taught app developer. Back in the early iPad era of 2011 and 2012, I was busy creating educational apps on my weekends (reinforcing my aforementioned nerd credentials), so the invitation felt like an unexpected yet mostly doable brief.

My supervisor and introduction to employment at our institution was an extraordinary mentor, gentle, humorous and deeply committed to his students, but it became apparent that he was under enormous pressure. Some of this came from ongoing medical challenges, but much of it stemmed from an ongoing clash with a senior leader of learning and teaching, who was not particularly fond of my supervisor's progressive and student-centred approach. This was my first real taste of university politics, though my supervisor was far too dignified to air such matters publicly. Only years later, long after I had finished my PhD, did I come to understand how difficult that period truly was for him. Tragically, the strain proved too much. My supervisor went on sick leave and asked me to take over his teaching responsibilities. He never came back, but we are still in contact.

It was a bittersweet twist of fate. My supervisor's absence opened the door for me to step into a larger role within the ICT team; an incredible opportunity born from someone else's burnout. Around that time, the entire ICT programme was under formal review, with staff, subjects and performance under the microscope. As a fledgling academic with plenty of naïveté, I initially accepted the official explanations as mixed evaluations and slowing research output, which many attributed to the long shadow cast by ongoing review. It was only later, through conversation beyond our immediate circle, that I understood the depth of animosity the then Director of Learning and Teaching held towards our team and just how consequential that could be. By the end of 2016, the ICT group was disbanded, and our subjects were cut. I remember thinking, with a mix of resignation and disappointment, that my brief academic adventure had probably come to an end. A long story short, it was purely by chance that I connected with Professor

Lorraine Graham, the head of the Learning Intervention academic group. After filling in for a colleague and co-teaching a semester with her, she then encouraged me to apply for a position in her team. Learning Intervention has been my home since the start of 2018.

Level 3 final boss battle: understanding the greater politics at play in decision-making while only having the limited perspective of a small professional network as a new staff member.

Level 3 life lesson power up: trying to become the sponge of institutional knowledge to better understand what is happening within your institution and who is really making the decisions (but networking is really difficult in some institutions!).

LEVEL 4: EQUIPPING MY 'MASK OF PROTECTION' TO MAKE PROGRESS BUT AT WHAT COST?

Once I had a new home, I threw myself into becoming part of the team. Most people in the group welcomed me warmly, working alongside colleagues who made me excited every morning to come into our office. But there was one long-standing staff member who seemed to find my presence more irritating than inspiring. At first, I took it to heart, thinking I must have done something wrong. These days, when I'm better regulated, I understand that I can't control other people's insecurities about the progress of their career, but that doesn't mean it doesn't sting. When things got particularly rough (snide comments, exclusionary silences, subtle eye-rolls) I'd remind myself of comedian Bill Hicks' immortal words: 'It's just a ride'. And so I rode it, masking my justice sensitivity and softening my edges to play the political game of social capital. To borrow from Patrick Swayze in the 1989 film Road House, the priority was to 'Be nice'. I learnt that being the 'cherry pie' version of myself, always smiling, agreeable, always 'I'm travelling well thanks', was a lot easier than showing how much the behaviour of this colleague was both hurtful and infuriating.

That mask turned out to be a useful little piece of career armour. It helped me form coalitions and, occasionally, win a few small victories. One of my earliest was convincing the faculty to fund and create a Low Impact Sensory Space, the first of its kind in any faculty at our university. It was both reassuring and a little disheartening: reassuring because something, anything, had actually happened, yet also disheartening because we were the least wealthy faculty and yet somehow the first to act. Still, it gave me the confidence (and political cover) to keep going, to step up for roles that mattered and to do so with some credibility. My time on the university's Digital Taskforce during the chaotic pivot to online learning in 2020, followed by my stint as Co-director of Student Experience, taught me that visibility comes with scrutiny and that people tend to confuse passion with ambition, as though enthusiasm itself is a form of aggressive power play.

This was also the era of what I jokingly call the academic Hunger Games; a period of shrinking budgets and positions, rising workloads and an atmosphere of 'don't complain' that masked collective exhaustion. Every success was both a relief and a risk, as I became more aware that some people only consider something successful when they have had a hand in it occurring. Yet somehow, amid the institutional theatre, I found purpose. I know this is a controversial statement, but masking kept me safe and gave me the space to quietly build supportive networks so I could feel safe to eventually unmask to more people. My experiences taught me to read the room, pick my battles and occasionally, to let the mask slip just enough to show 'the real me', a slightly battle-worn but ever-enthusiastic one, behind it all. I am under no illusion: masking often is detrimental (for example, see Miller et al., 2021), but I also believe that most neurodivergent academics are not working in communities where it is consistently safe to unmask.

Level 4 final boss battle: navigating colleagues with different values when there is a political power imbalance in the institution.

Level 4 life lesson power up: finding a way to survive through masking if needed, but also recognising that masking is never the ideal solution and has a cost.

LEVEL 5: NOT WANTING PEOPLE TO THINK I WAS USING CHEAT CODES

As a relatively early-career academic, I became increasingly aware that there is a fine line between being seen as capable and being seen as too ambitious and getting 'too much' career help. Visibility in universities can be complicated, and sometimes standing out invites more scrutiny than support. So I kept the 'cherry pie' mask firmly in place while trying not to appear as though I were climbing too fast. My transition from Co-director of Student Experience to Director of Professional and Continuing Education was a valuable lesson in managing both expectations and perceptions. The major project during this time was the much-needed revitalisation of our Master of Education programme, which had not kept pace with the significant demographic shifts in its student body. But in reality, how could it? This shift was not foreseen by anyone. Our Master of Education course has evolved from primarily serving domestic, in-service teachers to largely supporting international Chinese students, many in their early 20s with limited teaching experience and little familiarity with Australian education systems. These students were mostly eager and hardworking, but the course was never designed for their needs. Change was clearly necessary, but in academia, proposing change can sometimes be interpreted as a criticism of the past, which understandably makes people defensive.

In this context, diplomacy became an essential skill. I learnt that 'bringing people with you' often means balancing sensitivity for existing work with the need to move forward. The greatest challenge was not the redesign itself, but navigating the emotions and ambitions that surfaced around it. Academia can attract strong personalities, and leadership roles often bring those dynamics into sharp relief. There were times when the job felt as much about managing relationships as about managing projects, and moments when empathy and patience were more valuable than policy documents. The day three colleagues ended up in my office in tears, each for different reasons, I realised just how emotionally charged this change process really was for many. Still, amid the stress, I found opportunities for genuine collaboration and growth. It reinforced for me that progress in universities is possible, but it requires persistence, a healthy dose of empathy and the humility to recognise that every reform touches someone's sense of identity and purpose. Of course, there are things that I would do differently now, but I believe most people left feeling at least heard.

Level 5 final boss battle: working with people who think it should have been them in a leadership role.

Level 5 life lesson power up: making people think that they are an integral member of a successful team placates most people, most of the time.

[THE SECRET LEVEL: PLAYING PARALLEL GAMES IN NEURODIVERGENT-LED SPACES]

Among the constant political games that accompany an increasing profile within a university, I found two safe spaces where I could finally be my unmasked self. Both were neurodivergent-led spaces, places where I did not have to explain my ways of thinking or apologise for my intensity. It is important to emphasise that I had deep institutional support for the establishment of both of these spaces. The first was Next Level Collaboration, a social enterprise I co-founded with the wonderful Jess Rowlings, an openly autistic speech pathologist and researcher. Together, we created co-op gaming programs for neurodivergent children that focus on developing social capacity in a neurodiversity-affirming way. These programmes are facilitated by neurodivergent adults who are trained and supported by us to create environments where participants can feel genuinely understood. For me, Next Level Collaboration is not just a social venture; it is a community built on trust, humour and shared experience. Every session feels like an antidote to the performance culture of academia, a place where creativity and difference are not only accepted but celebrated.

The second space was built from the same spirit of defiant optimism, but on a much larger stage. Alongside my neurodivergent colleagues and co-editors of this book, Dr. Jessica Riordan and Dr. Sarah Timperley, I worked to establish the University of Melbourne Neurodiversity Project (see Riordan et al., 2024; Timperley et al., 2025 for further background on this journey). What started as a series of conversations about frustrations and possibilities emerging from a study we conducted in one faculty turned into a carefully crafted email to the Vice Chancellor, complete with a video explaining why the University needed to take neurodiversity seriously. To our surprise, he wrote back. That small act of acknowledgement opened a door that had long been closed, leading to the co-funding of the project through the Vice Chancellor's Strategic Initiative Advance Funding and the Faculty of Education. Together, we built an ambitious programme of research, workshops and advocacy to make the university a more inclusive place. Working with Jess and Sarah reminded me that courage is contagious and that collective action can shift even the most stubborn hierarchies.

Both of these spaces became my safe haven in the academic game, hidden worlds where I could recharge, find allies and reconnect with what makes this work worthwhile. They provide not just a professional purpose but also safety, friendship and genuine belonging. In these environments, I can unmask without fear, surrounded by people who understand what that means. The real challenge, of course, was learning to remask when stepping back into the neurotypically normed spaces of the university. To flatten my energy, soften my directness and translate my enthusiasm into something that would not be misunderstood. Yet, knowing that these parallel neurodivergent-led worlds existed made that transition sustainable (at least, so far). Even when I'm not in these spaces, their existence is a reminder that, while the academic game can be exhausting, there are still pockets of joy and authenticity for those with the social capital to carve them out.

Bonus-level final boss battle: being okay to re-mask when returning to a neurotypically normed community.

Bonus-level life lesson power up: there is joy in finding neurodivergent communities in which it is safe.

LEVEL 6: FINDING A NEW MENTOR AND BECOMING A MENTOR TO OTHERS

I find it to be a strange feeling of profound grief when people you have seen as your protectors and sponsors leave an institution. It doesn't seem to matter whether it is through retirement, a new opportunity elsewhere or, as has been the case for some of the mentors who have guided me, for health reasons. When these people leave, I feel exposed. I also feel adrift, like I have left something of importance somewhere and I just can't find it (which I'm sure is a familiar experience for my fellow ADHDers). The loss feels real. All neurodivergent academics, and really all academics, have heard horror stories about exploitative or toxic supervisory relationships. Praise be to Cat[1] that I have never had to endure that. I have known for some time that this transition was coming, and yet, even with that awareness, it has still had an emotional impact on how I see my place within the faculty. Losing a mentor is not just about losing a person, it is about losing the sense of safety

[1]Just to clarify, Cat is my non-denominational higher power of choice.

and affirmation that comes from knowing someone truly 'gets' you.

One of the unexpected joys of academic life, though, is realising that you eventually become that person for others. There is something deeply fulfilling about being able to offer the same care, encouragement and quiet sponsorship that once helped you find your footing. Mentoring does not need to be formal or grand; it can start with something as small as a coffee chat, an honest conversation about aspirations, or an invitation to join a grant team. Sometimes it is about giving someone a nudge of confidence; other times it is about standing behind them while they take a leap. I have come to see mentoring as a kind of resistance against neuronormative cultures, a way of keeping humanity alive within an institution that can so easily forget what that means.

Level 6 final boss battle: dealing with the unknown when a mentor and protector leaves.

Level 6 life lesson power up: there are usually good people around who want to help.

END CREDITS AND A PREVIEW OF THE SEQUEL

Looking back over this first episode of my academic game, I can see how each level brought lessons that shaped who I am and how I work within middle management. I have learned when to speak up and when to listen, how to build things that matter within systems not built for people like me, and how to find solidarity in unexpected places. Success means little without kindness, and progress, while often slow, feels possible when shared with the right people. These lessons, often shared through the generosity of others, have taught me to slow down at times. To act when necessary, to think more strategically and to allow me to be hopeful about what academia can still become for our broader neurodivergent community. This chapter marks the end of Episode 1 of my career, the early adventures of discovery, failure and finding my footing. Perhaps in another 10 years I will be ready to write Episode 2. I am well aware that there are people in my orbit, of all neurotypes, whose wisdom I will look to as I continue to grow, and I hope that, along the way, I can bring others with me as the adventure continues.

REFERENCES

Acevedo, S. M., & Stolz, S. (2024). On the misuses of neurodiversity: Critical approaches and counter-narratives. *Autism in Adulthood*. https://doi.org/10.1089/aut.2024.0016

Botha, M., Chapman, R., Giwa Onaiwu, M., Kapp, S. K., Stannard Ashley, A., & Walker, N. (2024). The neurodiversity concept was developed collectively: An overdue correction on the origins of neurodiversity theory. *Autism*, *28*(6), 1591–1594.

Dwyer, P. (2022). The neurodiversity approach(es): What are they and what do they mean for researchers?. *Human Development*, *66*(2), 73–92. https://doi.org/10.1159/000523723

Hayward, S. M., & Flower, R. L. (2025). A systematic review to move Australian disability employment forward for autistic people. *Review Journal of Autism and Developmental Disorders*, *12*(1), 151–162.

Kpolovie, P. J., Joe, A. I., & Okoto, T. (2014). Academic achievement prediction: Role of interest in learning and attitude towards school. *International Journal of Humanities Social Sciences and Education (IJHSSE)*, *1*(11), 73–100.

Miller, D., Rees, J., & Pearson, A. (2021). "Masking is life": Experiences of masking in autistic and nonautistic adults. *Autism in Adulthood*, *3*(4), 330–338.

Riordan, J., Timperley, S., O'Brien, C., Edwards, C., Murrihy, C., Harrison, M., & Mendus, A. (2024). Creating the conditions for inclusion: Investigating optimal physical spaces for supporting neurodivergent staff and postgraduate students. *Neurodiversity*, 2, 27546330241285353.

Timperley, S., Riordan, J., & Harrison, M. (2025). *"Being always visible means I'm never comfortable": An exploratory analysis of neurodivergent experiences of spaces and how they are utilised in a large Australian university*. https://doi.org/10.26188/30194923

9

IT DOESN'T GET ANY EASIER AT THE TOP (AT LEAST NOT YET)

SANDRA C. THOM-JONES

University of Wollongong, Australia

ABSTRACT

This chapter delves into the challenges faced by neurodivergent leaders in university and higher education settings, focusing on the experiences of a senior autistic member of a university leadership team. It explores this leader's decision to come out as autistic and the subsequent impact on their relationships within the team. Despite their senior position, the leader found that many of the tensions and barriers they experienced as an early-career academic persisted, including ongoing challenges of communication and understanding in a high-pressure environment. Coming out as autistic brought both positive and negative reactions from colleagues, highlighting the complexities of being neurodivergent in leadership roles. This chapter emphasises the crucial role of empathetic and supportive relationships in leadership. It demonstrates how having a supportive manager or team can significantly impact the well-being and effectiveness of a neurodivergent leader, even at a senior career stage. This chapter concludes with a call for more neurodivergent academics to pursue leadership roles, advocating for a more inclusive and understanding academic environment.

Keywords: Autistic; leadership; management; disclosure; academia

Source: Artwork by Melissa Vallence.
A Portrait of Sandra C. Thom-Jones.

INTRODUCTION

I don't think I ever consciously aspired to be a leader, but I have consistently stumbled into leadership positions from my first job in the public service to my most recent role as a Pro Vice-Chancellor.

Perhaps this tendency towards leadership roles is due in part to my innate inability to be a follower. My mother's favourite photo of me is a row of small girls doing ballet, all beautifully posed facing stage right, except for one standing with her arms crossed and facing stage left.

I commence this chapter with a brief snapshot of my leadership journey to give the context for what follows. I provide an overview of my experience of disclosing my autism diagnosis while in a senior leadership position and the ramifications of that disclosure (both positive and negative). I then reflect on some of the strengths of autistic people as leaders and conclude with my wish for the future. Throughout, I include reflections from people who have worked with me in my university leadership roles[1] because we can only be leaders if people choose to follow us.

A SNAPSHOT OF MY LEADERSHIP JOURNEY

My first full-time post-PhD academic job was at the University of Wollongong (UoW) in 2002, working for Prof. Don Iverson, who became my long-time boss and mentor. He hired me on a temporary contract to work on a research project and then into a standard academic role where I was teaching in the School of Public Health. Despite my entry-level role, Don encouraged me to apply for grants for research projects that I was interested in. I got my first Australian Research Council (ARC) Grant[2] in 2003 as co-investigator with Don and recruited a research assistant and PhD student. Later that year, I was appointed Associate Director of the Research Centre and promoted to Senior Research Fellow. In 2004, I was also appointed to the role of Associate Dean, Research for the Faculty of Health and Behavioural Sciences.

[1]When I was writing my most recent book, '*Autistics at Work*', I invited people who had worked with me since I commenced my first leadership role to respond to a survey on their experiences.

[2]The Australian Research Council Grant scheme is one of the two major national competitive research funding schemes offered by the Australian government (along with the National Health and Medical Research Council Grant scheme).

Later that year, I was awarded two more ARC Grants and a National Breast Cancer Foundation (NBCF) Grant, was promoted to Associate Professor and became a full-time researcher. At that point, I submitted an application to the university to set up my own research centre, with my mentor's blessing, and established the Centre for Health Initiatives. Over the next decade, I was awarded another 14 nationally competitive grants (10 as lead investigator) and more than 40 other grants and contract research projects. In 2007 I was promoted to Professor, and in 2014 to Senior Professor. Our centre grew rapidly, and by 2014 we had more than 20 staff, 26 full members, 80 Higher Degree Research students and an annual budget of $2.5 million (Jones & Phillipson, 2021).

Many people have commented on the speed of my progression through the ranks of academia, from Level A in 2002 to Level E in 2007. I attribute this to two things. The first is the strengths that I brought to my role as an autistic person – hyperfocus, work ethic, attention to detail, depth of interests and thirst for knowledge – which I will reflect on in more detail later in this chapter. The second was my good fortune in spending the majority of my academic career, and in particular this early period, in a supportive environment that recognised and valued my different ways of working, thinking and interacting. It was much later in my career that I came to learn that this level of acceptance and inclusiveness is not the norm in academia.

In 2014, I left UoW and moved to the Australian Catholic University, where I established and led a new research centre until 2017, when I was appointed to the role of Pro Vice-Chancellor, Engagement. Four years later, I moved to the role of Pro Vice-Chancellor, Research Impact. In 2023, I left the university sector.

Being an Openly Autistic Leader

When I was writing my book *Autistics at Work*, I reviewed the literature on autistic leadership. It didn't take long. I found a reasonable body of research on managing autistic employees, but only two articles that focused on autistic people as managers or leaders, both in autism-focused organisations.[3] One, published in 2019, was a case study of PAS Nederland, a consumer-run organisation by and for autistic adults (van den Bosch et al., 2019) and the other, published in 2024, reported on interviews with seven autistic leaders and four non-autistic leaders who worked with autistic people (Williams et al., 2024).

I was unable to identify any published research on autistic leaders in higher education. However, I am optimistic that this will change as there is a growing interest in this area, at least among graduate students, as evidenced by doctoral theses on autistic leadership (Roese, 2024; Spencer, 2025).

There are a few openly senior autistic leaders in the university sector, consistent with other disabilities. In Australia, a 2022 report found that there were no vice-chancellors, provosts or deputy vice-chancellors in any Australian university with a disability (including neurodivergence) disclosed on their official biography published on their employer's website or on their LinkedIn or Wikipedia profile (Harpur & Szücs, 2022); personal correspondence with the authors confirmed that, as a Pro Vice-Chancellor at the time, I was one of less than a handful in the next tier of university leadership with a disclosed disability. This is not to suggest that there are not senior university leaders who are autistic, but rather that those who are have chosen not to publicly disclose, do not have a diagnosis, or are unaware that they are autistic.

My own decision to publicly disclose was both sudden and widespread. The fact that I was autistic was an open secret within my work unit (more open than I realised, which I will discuss shortly), but I had not shared this information with the organisation per se, or with our external partners. Then I wrote an article for a national newspaper, expressing my ire about the way that

---

[3]I am excluding from this number offensive, ableist theoretical perspective pieces about 'autistic traits' such as this: 'Among other things, powerful people, and those with many autistic traits, tend to prefer solitary activities and are often aloof. Moreover, they are often rigid and socially insensitive, low on empathy and with low scores on the trait of agreeableness – and as a rule they do not have many friends. Both groups are also more self-centred than others, more honest, less submissive, more sensitive to slights, and with a stronger tendency to engage in abstract thinking' Overskeid, G. (2016).

some people use 'autistic' as an insult, in which I clearly identified that this was my own identity I was defending (Jones, 2019).

The Immediate Response to My Disclosure

The initial reaction to my disclosure was overwhelmingly positive, both within my organisation and beyond. Among my immediate work team, from those who had worked for me for over a decade to the newest members of the team, the response was predominantly congratulatory comments on the article. There were no expressions of surprise at what I thought would be a revelation to them. Over the following weeks and months, I came to learn that most of them had known, or suspected, my neurodivergence for many years – in some cases for longer than I had. One afternoon, as I was talking to a staff member who had joined my team 12 years earlier, initially as a research student, she informed me that the other students had briefed her on my autistic ways of working. I was relieved to discover that the briefing, in addition to mentioning the quirks in my body language and communication style, included references to my being an extremely supportive and caring supervisor who was committed to the career development of her team.

The reaction from my immediate supervisor was much the same, as was that of the majority of my colleagues. Those who hadn't already suspected my neurodivergence responded with smiles, nods and mutters of 'oh, well now that explains [insert whatever it was about my mannerisms or behaviours that puzzled them]'. Several asked questions about how autism impacted me and/or what they could do to support me.

I received many emails from autistic people who were working in academia, or in senior positions in other industries, thanking me for the article I had written – and, more broadly, for disclosing my diagnosis publicly. Some of these were colleagues or acquaintances, but the majority were strangers. Sadly, many of them commented that they had not disclosed at work due to concerns about autism stigma and the risk of negative impacts on their career prospects. I also received negative emails from strangers, expressing complete disbelief that I could be autistic, citing reasons such as 'because you have a job at a university' or 'because you are married'. Some were more deeply disturbing – in particular, the one asking me if I was interested in collaborating on a study into genetic screening for autism (presumably so that future generations could screen people like me out of existence).

But Then What Happened?

Within my own work unit, my decision to disclose continued to have only positive outcomes. I was able to make a number of environmental adjustments, which made working more comfortable and less draining. I felt comfortable to turn the overhead light off in my office, to request that the air conditioning vent over my desk be blocked and to bring my own desk chair to work.

I was able to communicate my needs in relation to communication and interaction in ways that were understood to be aspects of my autistic brain, rather than signs of unsociability. Instead of feeling pressured to eat in the communal lunch room, I was able to explain that I needed the time alone to decompress and recharge my batteries. Instead of constantly worrying that my emails might be interpreted as blunt or unfriendly (and thus spending hours agonising over their wording), I was able to explain to regular correspondents that I found communicating factual information easy but formulating appropriate pleasantries difficult.

Those who had wondered about my quirks now better understood them and were keen to support me in the workplace. An important flow-on effect was that my disclosure and subsequent changes to my work environment empowered other staff – both neurodivergent and neurotypical – to ask for the adjustments they needed. As one of my team noted in response to the survey on their experiences of working with me:

> *'Sandra was a great supervisor to me before disclosing, however, I felt when she went public in our wider team, it led to some fantastic reciprocal understandings in the wider team, and how we all worked together. There was learning for us all! Sandra was upfront*

> *about her neurodiversity (after disclosing) and grew in confidence with respect to reasonable adjustments in workplace functioning. This empowered me to seek support for my needs in the workplace.'*
>
> Source: *direct report ACU.*

Similarly, I was able to negotiate with my direct supervisor – who had little prior knowledge of autism but was keen to learn and to support me – for adjustments to my role and workload to make it more suited to my ways of working and to my interests. I was also given the go-ahead to develop an autism inclusion programme for the university, including a peer mentoring programme and a suite of resources for autistic students, professional development activities for staff and campus activities to increase autism acceptance and inclusion.

But it wasn't all positive. While the majority of people were supportive, I saw subtle – and sometimes not so subtle – shifts in the reactions of others. At the time of my disclosure, I had been through a protracted dispute with a staff member who reported to me, which had arisen out of a performance management process and was working with HR on a plan for the restructure of the organisational unit. I entered the meeting expecting a continuation of our previous discussion. What ensued, however, was a very one-sided conversation that concluded with a recommendation that the university provide me with a coach to work on my communication skills. At that point, I had been successfully managing teams of researchers for 15 years. I had consistently positive 360-degree evaluations and no history of communication problems in the workplace. Suddenly, I was faced with the assumption by HR that any conflict in the workplace must be due to deficits in my ability to communicate with my team. The only thing that had changed between those two meetings was my public disclosure that I am autistic.

How Did the Wheels Fall Off?

When my contract was due for renewal, I was unexpectedly advised only days before my scheduled interview that it had been put on hold to consider how my role could be 'reimagined'. Over the following months I repeatedly asked for updates, each time reminding the decision-maker of the impact of uncertainty on me as an autistic person. I became physically ill, taking several weeks of sick leave (unprecedented for me). More than four months later, I was told that I was being moved into a new role – a very important and prestigious role, but not one that I had sought or wanted (and one that involved disbanding my very productive and happy team). I moved into the role, and because it was important for the university and because of my (autistic) qualities of loyalty, integrity and strong work ethic, I filled the role successfully for two years.

This is just one example of what became clear was a pattern of disregarding my needs, while claiming that I was accepted and valued as an autistic person. It was a revelation to me, as someone who had thrived as a leader in academia, how much difference the lack of a supportive culture made to my capacity to function. The events of that period – including having my needs ignored, my team dispersed, and witnessing the constant political infighting and bullying experienced by my colleagues – led to a health collapse and thus my eventual decision to leave academia.

SHOULD AUTISTIC PEOPLE BE LEADERS?

The simple answer to this is 'Yes, BUT' – autistic people should aspire to leadership roles in organisations that truly value and support diversity, and our academic institutions should aspire to be these organisations that autistic people want to lead.

While it was not until some years into my leadership journey that I discovered I was autistic, and later still that I disclosed this to my organisation, I believe there are many things about autistic people that predispose us to – and make us ideally suited for – leadership roles.

We Know Stuff

In an ideal world, leaders should be those who know a great deal about the work of those they are leading (although I acknowledge that, particularly in academia, this is often not the case). Given our depth of interests, intense focus, and commitment to learning everything we can about topics we are passionate about, it makes sense that autistic people are often experts in their fields of endeavour.

Academia, when it works well, provides the ideal environment for autistic people to develop into leaders in their fields of expertise. In part, I fell into leadership because I was passionate about my area of research, and I had so many ideas about how to fill the gaps that I could see in the knowledge base and the commitment to keep working harder. Each time I had a new project, I needed to hire new staff to work on it, so my team grew.

> *'Sandra has a wealth of applied research skills, crossing different methodologies, and different stakeholder groups. This makes her an amazing mentor or boss if you're working in applied research. She understands stakeholder mapping, and how to align research goals with organisational imperatives that guide many of the clients we work with.'*
>
> Source: *direct report ACU.*

However, none of this would have happened without the support and encouragement of the leaders around me. I was extremely fortunate that both of my research centres were established within cultures where I had both direct managers and senior leaders who valued the work I was doing. I have seen many autistic researchers hampered by senior leaders and administrative structures that discourage junior academics from striking out on their own.

We Work Hard

A consistent finding of the research into autistic strengths in the workplace is that autistic people are conscientious and committed employees (Cope & Remington, 2022) who focus intently on their work, pay greater attention to detail, and make deliberate and consistent decisions (Griffiths et al., 2024). We tend to work hard, focusing deeply on the task at hand and not being distracted by small talk or office politics. The high levels of honesty and integrity that are common among autistic people make us diligent workers who are punctual, don't do personal tasks on work time, and only take sick leave if we are actually sick. Our attention to detail and drive for perfection – while this can at times irritate our neurotypical colleagues – means that we are committed to delivering work of the highest standard.

> *'Sandra was (and I'm sure still is) the hardest working person I knew, and seemed to have endless energy to give in the workplace. When she gave instruction it was straightforward – not blunt, but expectations were clear. My experiences post-working with Sandra have shown me that this quality is very rare. I thrive when I know expectations and I like clear instruction, so this leadership style worked for me. I felt that Sandra's passion for her work rubbed off on me, and it made me strive to work harder and want more for myself.'*
>
> Source: *direct report UoW.*

However, if unchecked, these excellent qualities can also be to our detriment. Like many autistic people, I have always had difficulties with boundaries in the workplace. When I commenced my career in academia, I felt so immensely grateful for the opportunity that I took on all tasks that were allocated to me, whether they were in my job description or not. I worked long hours in the office and longer hours at home in the evenings and on weekends, never considering saying no to a request or letting my supervisor know that I was overloaded (although my more observant and caring supervisors were apparently aware of it).

> *'Sometimes her overcommitment to help others meant she stretched herself and so compromised her own wellbeing and self-care.'*
>
> Source: *supervisor ACU.*

I earned a reputation for being reliable and someone who would always do what needed to be done. As I moved further up the leadership ladder, I found my problems with setting boundaries becoming even more problematic. I found myself supervising a large group of people, and I pedalled frantically to respond to their requests in a timely fashion so as not to delay their work. Then when they all left for the day, I started on the work that my manager (and his manager in turn) were expecting from me. Over the years this led to several periods of intense burnout; weekends and holidays were dedicated to sleeping and recovering rather than enjoying time with my family and friends.

We Care About Stuff

The common autistic characteristics of high moral values (Hartman & Hartman, 2024; Nocon et al., 2022) and commitment to social justice mean we are often the ideal candidate to lead teams and direct organisations in pursuit of endeavours that advance societal goals.

A consistent theme throughout my working life has been that the decisions I make about what work to do and how to do it are driven by my values. As a research leader, this has meant saying no to potentially lucrative opportunities (for example, when a multinational company offered me significant research funding) and taking on work that was seen by others as undesirable (for example, an underfunded project for an organisation supporting young people in rural areas).

This is what makes the work we do meaningful, for me and for my team. At the beginning of each year, I engaged in annual planning sessions with my team, where we would discuss what we had achieved over the last year and what we wanted to achieve for the next year (and beyond). This ensured a shared sense of ownership of, and commitment to, our goals and the opportunity for new ideas to be tabled. It also kept me (and others) honest, so we didn't take on new projects that didn't fit with our vision and overall goals.

> *'Sandra is a very passionate and committed advocate and her enthusiasm for her work is infectious; many autistic individuals have a strong social justice drive and evident in the positive change Sandra has created at ACU for autistic and neurodivergent students and staff. She is also committed to liaising with staff and the community to increase awareness and understanding of autism, which will make it easier for future students and staff who may still be developing their self-advocacy skills.'*
>
> Source: *direct report ACU.*

However, this can also make leadership challenging for autistic people if we find that our values are inconsistent with those of the organisation; or, perhaps more likely, in conflict with the more self-serving goals of some other leaders in the organisation.

> *'The hardest thing about working for Sandra is witnessing the terrible toll her role takes on her mental and physical health. Seeing Sandra hospitalised on several occasions for conditions related to stress was heartbreaking for me.'*
>
> Source: *direct report ACU.*

We Care About People

The myth that autistic people lack empathy, while largely disproven, continues to influence neurotypical perceptions of our interactions in workplaces as well as the broader community. The reality is that autistic people are often highly empathetic, but we express our empathy in different ways (and we may not pick up on non-spoken cues from non-autistic colleagues). Other authors in this book have discussed the double empathy problem, so I will not re-explain it here, other than to say that, when both neurotypes are aware of the communication differences, relationships are far more productive.

My non-autistic colleagues would often comment, with some surprise – and I suspect a smidge of envy – on the level of loyalty and commitment in my team. With a few rare exceptions, the people who worked for me were intensely loyal and would go above and beyond for the team and the project. This was evidenced when I changed universities in 2014, which involved moving interstate, and six of my staff relocated with me.

What did I do to earn this loyalty? I was unflinchingly loyal to *them*. I have learned from my own harsh experiences just how much impact a leader can have on the culture of an organisational unit or a whole organisation. Like most autistic people, I have little interest in hierarchy or politics. I try to make sure that I consistently model a culture of openness and inclusion, where staff feel safe to be themselves, to speak up, to share ideas, to admit to vulnerabilities and mistakes and to celebrate successes. I also believe that a leader takes the blame and shares the glory.

> *'I didn't report directly into Sandra, but as the head of my organisational unit I found her to be incredibly people-focused. I always had a sense that Sandra would 'go in to bat' for her team members and that she was protective of, and loyal to, her people. I remember an instance where I had forgotten to deliver a task that I was assigned for a senior executive outside of our team. When this person followed up with Sandra, I admitted to her I had forgotten the task. Instead of letting the executive know I had dropped the ball, she responded to them to say that we were working on it and it would arrive soon, without ever laying any blame on me.'*
>
> Source: *indirect report ACU.*

> *'Personally, I admire Sandra greatly. Sandra treats all (no matter their position, title or seniority) with respect and as equals. She has the ability to empower her staff in the respectful way she collaborates. She has always encouraged me to develop my skills and responsibilities in the workplace. She has been a wonderful support to*

me personally and professionally. Sandra has been a brilliant advisor at times providing sound advice and perspectives. She has a gift of listening and empathizing. Working with Sandra has been a gift for me personally, and is definitely one thing I cherish while with the organisation.'

Source: *colleague ACU.*

MY THREE WISHES

When I look back on my career as a university leader, I feel great pride in the things that I accomplished. What stands out for me is not the grants I won or the papers I published (although those were pretty cool), but the staff I mentored and supported who went on to achieve great things in their own careers. I am eternally grateful to the people who supported me to be my authentic self in the workplace, even before my diagnosis, and recognised the strengths that I brought as an autistic leader. Looking back, I have three wishes for myself, and looking forward, I have three wishes for academia.

For Myself

First, I wish that I had disclosed earlier so that I had not endured decades of masking before I allowed myself to truly be 'me' in the workplace. Second, I wish that my good fortune in having an autism-friendly culture, which I enjoyed for 20 years in academia, had continued to the end of my academic career. Third, I wish I had set boundaries for myself and not been so self-critical of my challenges; it was not until I collected data for *Autistics at Work* that I discovered those I worked with didn't share my reservations about my people skills.

'I am going to guess that Sandra would list one of her challenges as people management. I know this because she would often comment to me that she wasn't good at people management and apologise for things that

> *happened in relation to people and managing staff. However, I actually think Sandra was the best people manager in our team. Other managers often "talk the talk" but she actually "walks the walk" – she offers good advice and support, helps you solves problems and, most importantly, values the opinions of her staff, takes feedback on board and empowers people to do the best they can at their job. Despite this, I think Sandra doubts herself. At times, I noticed her apologising for things that I am certain weren't her fault (were actually things other managers had done) because she assumed they were good at people management, and she was not. Maybe we all didn't tell her enough that we felt this way.'*
>
> Source: *indirect report ACU.*

For Academia

First, I wish that all academic institutions would provide comprehensive autism awareness and acceptance programs for staff and students, raising understanding of both the challenges and strengths of autistic people and providing genuinely inclusive working environments. Second, I wish that every autistic person in academia could have the kind of support network that I had for the majority of my career, with both direct supervisors and Vice-Chancellors who are genuinely committed to inclusion (and access to guidance and corrective action where this is not the case). Third, I wish that autistic people currently in senior academic roles could be encouraged and supported to disclose – with genuine assurance that this will not lead to discrimination or harm. We need to be visible for the future autistic leaders of academia (some of whom have written chapters in this book) who are looking to us to show that autistic people can and should aspire to leadership roles.

REFERENCES

Cope, R., & Remington, A. (2022). The strengths and abilities of autistic people in the workplace. *Autism in Adulthood*, *4*(1), 22–31. https://doi.org/10.1089/aut.2021.0037

Griffiths, A. J., Torres, R., Delgado, R., Hurley-Hanson, A. E., Giannantonio, C. M., Walrod, W., Maupin, Z., & Brady, J. (2024). Understanding unique employability skill sets of autistic individuals: A systematic review. *Journal of Employment Counseling*, *61*(2), 74–104. https://doi.org/10.1002/joec.12223

Harpur, P., & Szücs, B. (2022, 22 Feb). Where are the leaders with a disability in higher education?. *Higher Education*. https://www.timeshighereducation.com/campus/where-are-leaders-disability-higher-education

Hartman, L., & Hartman, B. (2024). An ethical advantage of autistic employees in the workplace [Brief Research Report]. *Frontiers in Psychology*, *15 – 2024*. https://doi.org/10.3389/fpsyg.2024.1364691

Jones, S. C. (2019, July 9). Autism, a neurotype not an insult. *Sydney Morning Herald*. https://www.smh.com.au/national/autism-a-neurotype-not-an-insult-20190620-p51zt6.html

Jones, S. C., & Phillipson, L. (2021). Centre for Health Initiatives, Wollongong, Australia. In C. Fourali & J. French (Eds.), *The Palgrave Encyclopedia of Social Marketing*. Palgrave Macmillan.

Nocon, A. S., Roestorf, A., & Menéndez, L. M. G. (2022). Positive psychology in neurodiversity: An investigation of character strengths in autistic adults in the United Kingdom in a community setting. *Research in Autism Spectrum Disorders*, *99*, 102071. https://doi.org/10.1016/j.rasd.2022.102071

Overskeid, G. (2016). Power and Autistic Traits [Hypothesis and Theory]. *Frontiers in Psychology*, *7–2016*. https://www.frontiersin.org/journals/psychology/articles/10.3389/fpsyg.2016.01290

Roese, K. (2024). *Measurement of leadership among autistic adults*. California State University.

Spencer, B. R. (2025). *Neurodiverse leadership: A phenomenological Study of leaders with autism in marketing*. Alliant International University.

van den Bosch, K. E., Krzeminska, A., Song, E. Y., van Hal, L. B. E., Waltz, M. M., Ebben, H., & Schippers, A. P. (2019). Nothing about us, without us: A case study of a consumer-run organization by and for people on the autism spectrum in the Netherlands. *Journal of Management and Organization*, *25*(4), 464–480. https://doi.org/10.1017/jmo.2018.54

Williams, N., Bragger, J., & Myszko, Z. (2024). (Neuro)Diversifying organizations: The case for developing autistic leaders. *Consulting Psychology Journal*, *76*(1), 1–19. https://doi.org/10.1037/cpb0000272

FURTHER READING

Thom-Jones, S. (2022). *Growing in to Autism* (p. 2025). Melbourne University Press.

Thom-Jones, S. (2025). *Autistics in Academia: Narratives of work, adversity, and achievement from around the world*. Cambridge University Press.

Thom-Jones, S. (2025). *Autistics at Work*. Melbourne University Press.

10

WHERE DIFFERENCE BELONGS: VIGNETTES FROM A GLOBAL NEURODIVERGENT RESEARCH COMMUNITY

SARAH TIMPERLEY[a], MICHAEL ARHIN-ACQUAAH[b], MU-YEN CHAN[c], CHRIS EDWARDS[d], AIMEE FLETCHER[e], INGA KOOPS[f], KUN-RONG LI[g], SALOME MUNYENGERWI[h], JESS ROWLINGS[i] AND ARI STAR[j]

[a]The University of Melbourne, Australia
[b]GIRES (Gender Identity Research and Education Society), UK
[c]University of Toronto, Canada
[d]Autism Spectrum Australia, Australia and Griffith University, Australia
[e]University of Glasgow, UK
[f]University of Southern Queensland, Australia
[g]Taiwan Youth with Disability Association, Taiwan and National Taiwan Normal University, Taiwan
[h]Reseacher and Community Mental Health Advocate, Zimbabwe
[i]The University of Melbourne, Australia and Next Level Collaboration, Australia
[j]Macquarie University, Australia

ABSTRACT

This final chapter shares stories of finding community written by neurodivergent researchers who are early in their research journey or who research outside of a university structure. The following nine vignettes explore perspectives from neurodivergent researchers from around the world. These vignettes are organised through four overarching themes that come through in each story: (1) the positive impacts of neurodiversity-affirming research and neurodivergent researchers, *(2)* the importance of online spaces for finding and building community, *(3)* becoming the mentor I needed *and (4)* finding identity through community and self-discovery. *Despite different cultures and experiences of diagnosis, support and acceptance, all authors shared a strong passion for research that works together with the community to shape the future and a desire to make the world better for everyone.*

Keywords: Neurodiversity-affirming research; building community; mentoring; neurodivergent identity; self-discovery; online communities; neurodiversity around the globe

INTRODUCTION

Thus far, the authors of this book have shared their experiences of working within higher education, including many of the challenges they have had to survive as neurodivergent researchers. In this final chapter, we focus on finding community to provide what we hope is a pathway towards thriving as an academic. To conclude this book on a note of optimism for better possible futures, we wanted to highlight that there are places and spaces where people are finding ways to feel a sense of belonging through connecting with other people who have walked a similar path. We asked neurodivergent researchers from around the world to share their experiences of community building via writing short vignettes. While these are thematically grouped, each reflection stands on its own as a small but important strand of that author's story.

Each author was asked to write about finding community in research, highlighting the many paths that can be taken to find others who make us feel seen and accepted. Many authors share their passion to continue fighting for inclusion beyond their own,

Source: Artwork by Melissa Vallence.
A Depiction of the Contributors to This Chapter.

to support neurodivergent and disabled communities, and to make the world a better place for generations to come. We believe these vignettes demonstrate the power neurodivergent people can have when we find each other, work together and have systems and spaces that better support our needs.

THEME 1: THE POSITIVE IMPACT OF NEURODIVERGENT RESEARCH AND RESEARCHERS

Within the vignettes were shared experiences of the positive impact that neurodiversity-affirming research and researchers can have on developing a sense of belonging. The first two authors speak to the importance of finding this research in places where neurodiversity is less understood, while the third reflects on how an inclusive research environment made her feel accepted as a neurodivergent researcher from the beginning of her academic journey.

Knowing Through Difference: A Dyslexic Perspective on Neurodiversity and Collective Belonging – Kun-Rong Li (He/Him)

> I am a person with dyslexia. Growing up in Taiwan's exam-oriented education system, I struggled with memorisation, recitation, and writing all the time, so I often ranked at the bottom of my class. Although I've reached a certain level of writing competence, I still struggle with omitting words and making spelling mistakes. While I face many challenges, this experience has also brought me many invaluable insights.
>
> In Taiwan, there is little academic discussion of neurodiversity, and few corresponding communities exist. Most people are not familiar with the concept. Whether in educational services or medical diagnosis, the dominant approach to learning disabilities adopts a medical model, focusing on remediation and supplementing the individual's difficulties. Consequently, most people with learning disabilities must navigate and understand their challenges on their own.
>
> My relationship with neurodiversity originated in the university Resource Centre. All universities in Taiwan are equipped with a Resource Centre, which not only provides students with reasonable accommodations

but also serves as a space for social interaction. In the Resource Centre, I met many peers like myself, and we shared our different experiences. This process led us to deeper reflection on questions like: 'How are disabilities defined?', 'Why is this identity stigmatized?'.

Together with these peers, I formed deep friendships. We began to read, reflect, and engage with ideas such as the social model of disability (Oliver & Barnes, 2012) and the politics of difference (Young, 1990). The social model clarified how people come to be defined as 'in need of help' not because of individual impairments, but because society is structured around nondisabled norms. It also revealed how state institutions label those affected as disabled, reinforcing stigmatised identities. At the same time, we came to value the forms of strength that emerge within communities through solidarity, shared identity, and mutual care. These insights showed us that acknowledging differences – and using that recognition as the basis for dialogue and advocacy – can open up more inclusive social and political possibilities.

As we continued to learn and reflect, we began to see our disabilities as meaningful parts of who we are. This understanding led us to establish the Taiwan Youth with Disability Association, through which we organised camps and forums that created spaces for disabled youth to express themselves and share their experiences.

Our community members represent a wide range of backgrounds, including wheelchair users, people with vision and hearing impairments, and of course, our neurodivergent peers. Although some of our neurodivergent peers may not face limitations due to environmental or physical barriers, we all share the experience of being socially marginalised. These interactions allowed me to better understand and embrace my own disability identity. When my peers see me missing or misspelling words, they joke about, 'The disability is manifesting!' However, the true meaning behind this is that here, any disability or trait is accepted, and everyone recognises your disability.

Through this continuous process of connecting with my disabled peers, I gradually accepted my disability identity and began to interact with others openly in that capacity. This acceptance spurred me to pursue further research and advocacy, sharing the experiences of more neurodivergent individuals. As a result of this journey, I am no longer ashamed of these traits. I hope my very existence shows the public the diverse tapestry of society, where every person – including individuals whose brain operates differently – can participate in life equally.

From Isolation to Reimagining: Finding My Neurodivergent Place in Academia – Salome Munyengerwi (She/Her)

I identify myself at the nexus of lived experience, advocacy, and research. I grew up looking after an epileptic mother in a culture that interpreted her condition as mental illness. This experience reflects what studies in Zimbabwe have documented: epilepsy is frequently misunderstood and associated with supernatural or psychiatric explanations, which contributes to stigma, delayed treatment, and isolation for families (Ngwende, 2020; Mutanana et al., 2020). I now help my aunt look after an autistic brother. These experiences were a hard lesson early on in seeing how the systems fail people who think and learn differently. My volunteer work at Nduna Girls in Zimbabwe, mentoring teens with diverse learning needs was where theory met practice. It was one thing to have grown up seeing my mother and brother failed by systems; it was another to stand beside these bright, determined girls and see the same story repeating itself. I witnessed firsthand how rigid curricula and a lack of resources stifled their potential.

This experience cemented my understanding that neurodivergence is not the barrier; the barrier is an environment unwilling to adapt. Through hands-on mentoring, I learned the transformative power of small, personalized adjustments, a different way of explaining a concept, a quiet space to complete work, or simply the affirmation that their way of thinking was not wrong, but unique. This reinforced my conviction that true inclusion is a dual mandate: it requires both top-down systemic change and grassroots, personal advocacy. Though I'm not professionally diagnosed, I self-identify and self-advocate from within the neurodivergent population and advocate for neurodivergent thinking and being. To me, that means the appreciation of different thinking and communication styles, and their establishment as strengths, rather than deficits.

My journey to belonging in academia has been long but transformative. Alone, I would say, was the feeling I lived with, especially being in Zimbabwe with aspirations to conduct research in Australia. The literature seemed predominantly to frame neurodivergence in narrow and medicalising terms; I thus wondered if my thoughts meant anything. All this changed when I began connecting with neurodivergent thinkers online. I remember coming across the 'Double Empathy Problem'. This idea, that communication breakdowns are mutual and never the deficit of a single neurodivergent individual changed my life. It reframed my entire life story. It was no longer that my mother or the girls I mentor were 'hard to reach'; it was that the world had failed to learn how to listen to them. This concept gave me the words to articulate the core of the isolation I had seen and felt, and it turned my confusion into crystal clear purpose. Invitations to participate in neurodivergent projects, like this one, have been incredibly affirming. It comforts me that my story, and stories like mine from Africa, not only belong in the academy but they are needed to reimagine it.

Finding this community has been the final, crucial piece in a journey that began in my childhood home. The through-line of my life, from navigating the dangerous misunderstandings around my mother's epilepsy to supporting my autistic brother to mentoring the brilliant girls at Nduna Girls has consistently shown me that our systems are designed for a narrow range of minds. I have seen firsthand how a rigid educational approach can extinguish a spark in a student who simply learns differently. I have felt the devastating cost when communication fails not due to a lack of trying but a lack of understanding. It is from this lived reality that my planned doctoral research on neurodivergent inclusion in schools is born. This work is not an abstract intellectual exercise; it is the necessary next step in a lifetime of advocacy. It is a commitment to translating the painful lessons from my mother's story and the hopeful lessons from my mentoring into actionable change. It is fuelled by the community of scholars that inspires me, and it is a promise to ensure that the next generation of neurodivergent children in Zimbabwe and beyond will be met not with misunderstanding but with celebration. Being connected to other neurodivergent academics reminds me that I am not alone in this fight, and together, we can reimagine education as a space where every kind of mind can not only belong but truly thrive.

These first two stories discuss how finding neurodivergent and disability research and community shape both an understanding of self and others and a drive towards making the world better for others. The final vignette in this section comes from someone who knew her identity before starting research and entered the kind of neurodiversity-affirming environment that Salome and Kun-Rong are creating in their own ways. Even in an inclusive environment, Ari has still found a neurodivergent community and the desire to improve things for others as a huge drive in her research.

Autistic Almost Academic – Ari Star (She/Her)

I am a passionate autistic autism research assistant and current Master of Research Student. As of recently, I am also a casual academic tutor for an inclusive education unit delivered to pre-service teachers. As well as being autistic, I have a form of dysautonomia, which means my autonomic nervous system struggles to regulate my blood pressure and heart rate, causing headaches, dizziness, and a rapid pulse. These symptoms worsen when I get too hot, and as an autistic person my temperature regulation is already quite poor. In addition to regulating physical symptoms, I also need to manage my exposure to light and sound, as both can trigger headaches and blurred vision, especially when my dysautonomia symptoms are already increased. In addition to this, I also have narcolepsy, which causes intrusive sleep, and results in me often needing to work on a different schedule, as I am most alert in the afternoon and evening when my medication is most effective.

I was diagnosed with Asperger's syndrome when I was nine, so I have grown up knowing I am autistic rather than discovering it as an adult which is common in the autism research community. Entering a neuro-affirming research space already aware of my diagnosis has made it easier for me to describe myself openly as an autistic autism researcher. I am grateful that I began connecting with a supportive neurodivergent community early in my career, starting with a placement working for an autism research team as part of my undergraduate degree. Through this work experience I discovered that I thoroughly enjoy the methodical process of researching. Working with the neurodivergent team who taught me so much about autism (and, therefore, about myself), ultimately inspired me to shift from my original career plan of disability policy and begin working towards starting a research career. Soon after the placement, I took my first steps in my research career as an 'almost-academic', working as a casual Research Assistant for one of the autism researchers. This role has allowed me to connect with dozens of other neurodivergent academics through research projects, community of practice groups, advisory committees, conferences, and online networks. While I do only work casually in academia at the moment, I am very excited to do my PhD and graduate to become an 'official' researcher with more autonomy around the projects I work on.

One of the greatest benefits of having a neurodivergent community within academia is the opportunity to collaborate with others who share my enthusiasm for research. I often demonstrate an intense and sustained focus on my areas of interest, and I find it very motivating to see this reflected in other neurodivergent researchers.

I have found that besides the support provided by members of the neurodivergent research community, fellow tutors who are also neurodivergent are often a good sounding board for concerns that arise in my teaching role. For example, when provided with unstructured material that I need to teach, discussing

> it with a neurodivergent colleague who processes information similarly to me can help 'translate' the content into a format I can understand. This not only helps me navigate the material but also fosters a sense of connection and shared understanding that I find deeply supportive.
>
> While it is incredibly motivating to see the autistic research community using experiential knowledge to increase understanding of our challenges, as well as the assets we bring to the academic space, I wish to acknowledge my privilege in experiencing a largely positive academic journey so far. This may in part reflect both the neurodivergent-affirming nature of my research focus and the early stage of my career, which has limited my exposure to other fields which may be less supportive. With this in mind, I am deeply inspired by the dedication of the autistic research community, who continue to produce research conducted *with* and *for* autistic people. It gives me hope that our collective efforts will lead to lasting change, fostering an academic community that is truly accessible, especially for those whose journeys have not been as easy as mine.

Engaging with affirming research and working with neurodivergent researchers can have an immensely positive impact on members of our community. It is worth noting that while Ari, who experienced an inclusive environment, happened to come from a Western country (Australia), the construction of this section does not mean to imply that Australia is necessarily 'better' at inclusion; indeed, many Australian scholars (and others around the world) have reported a mix of inclusionary and exclusionary experiences at universities (e.g. Mellifont, 2023).

Rather, these stories showed that pockets of inclusion can exist anywhere, whether that is a particularly inclusive university, a group of disabled scholars sharing ideas, a school, online communities, or a single person determined to advocate for others.

These stories also illustrate the importance of the work of neurodivergent and disabled scholars, as Kun-Rong and Salome discuss how discovering the social model of disability and the double empathy problem (Milton, 2012) helped re-conceptualise their understanding of themselves and their communities.

THEME 2: THE IMPORTANCE OF ONLINE SPACES FOR NEURODIVERGENT CONNECTION

A multitude of things can stand in the way of in-person connection, from culture to physical distance to sensory challenges to pandemics. The following authors have both reflected on how important it was for them to find community in online spaces due to the COVID-19 pandemic lockdowns, difficulty finding neurodivergent colleagues because people are not 'out', and primarily working from home.

Finding Community, or Community Finding You: Reflections on the Importance of Joining and Establishing Neurodivergent Researcher Communities – Aimee Fletcher (She/Her)

> When I started my PhD in October 2020, remotely from my bedroom due to the ongoing lockdowns due to the COVID Pandemic, I quickly realised the importance of community. Not just of other PhD candidates and Early Career Researchers (ECR), but of fellow autistic researchers who could relate and share their experiences. During the early years of doctoral and post-doctoral research, I, like most researchers in this situation, was finding my feet as a researcher. Part of that process involved looking to others with a little more experience to help shape my own practices. I could find other PhD researchers fairly easily, both within my local and the online PhD community, but I found it harder to find openly neurodivergent PhD and ECRs. At the time, I realised this was likely due to

neurodivergent researchers not necessarily feeling safe to openly share their experiences outside of closed groups, for fear of discrimination or their openness impacting their own careers, but it fed that feeling of isolation during a time that was isolating for everyone.

I decided that I would start sharing my experiences of being neurodivergent in academia openly. At first posting about my research experiences, particularly finding my feet and what worked for me that perhaps wasn't the standard approach other 'neurotypical' researchers would take, on Twitter (now X). Over time, the number of people that followed me and responded to say thanks or share their own tips grew. I received messages from people who were not yet confident to share in a public space that they identify as being neurodivergent, but felt that my sharing helped them to feel more confident sharing in their personal groups. Before I knew it, I was speaking about being 'Autistic in Academia' in my university's PhD welcome conference, making the video available online afterwards, then holding in-person 'Autistic Autism Researcher' meet-ups at Autscape (an Autistic-led, neurodivergent majority annual conference in the UK) which was far more well-attended than I could have imagined. At last, I had found a community that made me feel welcome and supported.

I have now completed my PhD, which was all about making museums accessible for neurodivergent adults through participatory practices, and it would not have been possible without creating and finding neurodivergent community members. I have made lifelong friends as well as collaborators who make me feel safe and a wonderful sense of belonging. While I do not work in a traditional academic position currently, I continue to support, mentor and engage in the neurodivergent research community online and at conferences as these spaces continue to feel like home to me.

Being able to continue to connect with neurodivergent researchers online has enabled me to not only collaborate in research projects I otherwise may not have had access to outside of academia, it has also let me develop the friendships I have made at international conferences. For example, I met Dr TC Waisman, a fantastic openly Autistic and Indigenous researcher based in Canada while attending the INSAR conference in Melbourne in 2024. When I arrived at the conference, I did not attend with anyone and felt anxious about whether this would be a space I would feel safe or find many other Autistic researchers. I met TC at an informal meal for Autistic researchers, organised through a WhatsApp group set up by members of INSAR's Autistic Researcher's Committee to help us to find each other, and we became fast friends. TC, and other Autistic researchers such as Monique Botha, took me under their wing during what was my first international conference. I had never flown alone, never mind a long-haul flight, and I found a safe place in our friendship. Since this conference, many of us have remained in contact in some form, and the continued tradition of organising WhatsApp spaces for neurodivergent researchers to join in advance has made me feel more confident attending and being openly Autistic at conferences.

Remote, But Not Alone – Chris Edwards (He/Him)

My name is Chris, and I am an autistic autism researcher. My work sits between community and academia: I'm based in a national autism-specific not-for-profit, and I also supervise three PhD students through an academic affiliation. One of the things that makes my work actually doable is that it's fully remote. I learned a long time ago that open-plan offices give me too much anxiety and sensory overwhelm to function, let alone thrive. Working from home lets me focus on the parts of my job I care about most, like qualitative research with autistic adults. I'm especially drawn to projects where I recognise parts of my own life in the stories people share. That connection isn't a problem to me, it's what makes my work meaningful.

My pathway to community was shaped by being alone a lot of the time. I did my whole PhD from home. The university offered me a desk in a shared office with a dozen other research students, but as soon as I walked in that room I thought, 'NOPE, this is not for me'. What made the biggest difference was being part of the Autism CRC community (a national autism research collaboration in Australia). Without that link, I honestly don't think I'd have connected with anyone during my PhD.

When I started my current research role in 2022, our communications advisor suggested I join Twitter/X. Back then it felt like a safe and active space to meet other autistic and neurodivergent researchers, both in Australia and overseas. Because my role is fully remote and my colleagues are in other states, online spaces became my main way of building professional relationships and finding people whose work and experiences resonated with mine. I don't really use Twitter/X anymore, but I stayed in touch with many of those people and now LinkedIn is my main space for professional community.

Finding other neurodivergent academics has changed everything for me. As an autistic person researching autism, there isn't a clean line between the personal and the professional, how could there be? Community

> gives me people who get both, who understand what the work involves and what living it feels like. Having colleagues I can message to vent, celebrate, or just say 'is it just me?' makes a real difference. My wife is also neurodivergent and incredibly supportive, but she's not in academia. Having a network of people who share both parts of my life (neurodivergence and research) gives me a kind of connection I didn't realise I was missing.

Aimee and Chris both discuss different reasons for turning to online spaces for a sense of community, but both have found these spaces incredibly important. Neurodivergent academics, researchers, university staff, and students across the globe have reported reluctance to disclose their neurodivergence to universities (e.g. Kennedy et al., 2025; Mellifont, 2023; Riordan et al., 2024; Sarchet, 2024). Aimee's experiences that it can be challenging to find openly neurodivergent researchers in person makes sense in this context, and illustrates the importance of creating safe spaces for those who do not want their identities shared.

As Chris discussed, open plan office environments are a source of anxiety and sensory overwhelm for him; a sentiment shared by many other neurodivergent people (Thorpe et al., 2024; Timperley et al., 2025). As such, many neurodivergent employees have expressed a preference for remote or hybrid work (Das et al., 2021). These stories share how connection does not have to be in person, and show the vital role of online spaces in building and maintaining community.

THEME 3: BECOMING THE MENTOR I NEEDED

The next two authors share how becoming mentors was crucial in finding their own identities and creating spaces where they (and their younger counterparts) can thrive in a world that isn't always hospitable.

Academia: A Hide and Seek Journey of Neurodivergent Identity – Inga Koops (She/Her)

Academia has hosted a long, complex journey of hide and seek for my neurodivergent identity. Across several degrees and many years, I navigated university while masking the challenges I faced as an unidentified Autistic student. The relentless pressure to fit in, keep up, and push through the sensory onslaught of academic life led to burnout, painful setbacks, and a car crash that could easily have taken my life.

My story of hiding began to shift during my master's research, when I became a mentor for neurodivergent university students. Mentoring sparked curiosity, renewal, and purpose creating safe spaces that encouraged neurodivergent ways of being. Through supporting neurodivergent undergraduates, I began to unveil my own neurodivergent identity and the parts of myself I once misunderstood, believed were broken, and felt compelled to hide.

Listening to their stories was like hearing echoes from my own undergraduate years. For me, sensory chaos was a constant challenge – the scratching of pens, humming fluorescent lights, and the thick air filled with perfume and body heat made focusing difficult. When participating in group discussions and oral presentations, I often froze despite knowing the material well. Meanwhile, the pressure of deadlines collided with executive functioning challenges, making organisation and planning a daily struggle. This recognition inspired my current PhD research into participatory methods and transforming support systems for neurodivergent folks across all levels of academia.

What started for me as mentoring evolved into a passion for building community – a mutual exchange of learning, support, and solidarity among neurodivergent academics at all career stages. I believe these connections will challenge marginalisation and foster collective strength, reshaping cultures within academia to value and embrace diversity in how people think, work, and relate.

This journey of coming out of hiding continues to unfold, entwining identity with research and advocacy. I am still navigating disclosure in wider networks, but my drive is clear: to be the mentor I once needed, confronting stigma, misinformation, and structural barriers. Along the way, I have found glimpses of true belonging – an experience beyond anything I had known before.

Slowly, I am shedding masks and limiting scripts, redefining how I show up in the academic world. No longer striving to fit a system never designed for me, I stand alongside brilliant colleagues to challenge entrenched perceptions and build spaces where diverse ways of being and working are recognised and embraced.

What started as hiding has transformed into seeking and finding belonging. I am beginning to see myself not as flawed or out of place, but as part of a vibrant neurodivergent academic community, driving change and building cultures of solidarity where we can thrive.

Next Level Collaboration: Accidental Entrepreneurship That Changed the Game – Jess Rowlings (She/Her)

When I reached the end of my formal education I wasn't sure what I wanted to do as a career. I found most industry work environments challenging, if not exhausting, and for most of my formative years I never felt like I was good at much other than getting high grades at school. There were so many things that seemed to come easily to everyone except me, but because of my gender and academic achievement it was never considered that I might be neurodivergent until I reached adulthood. I had always enjoyed learning though, with my (what I now know to be) autistic side wanting to find out as much information as possible about my areas of interest and my ADHD craving the excitement and novelty of new knowledge. Looking back, it seems only natural that I ended up choosing academia as a career – a field that encourages original contributions and continual knowledge development in rather specific areas.

Not long into my first year of academia, I received an email inviting me to co-found a startup called Next Level Collaboration. The idea was brilliant; a research-based program that uses cooperative video games to help build collaborative teamwork skills, while also creating job opportunities for neurodivergent young adults. I never thought of myself as entrepreneurial, but I loved the idea of leading a project based around two of my biggest interests, neurodivergence and video games. I also knew through my personal and professional experiences that so many neurodivergent children needed a place where they could build social connections and belong to a community that celebrates their strengths and interest in gaming. Not wanting to let anyone try and talk me out of entering the startup world, I instantly responded with a big 'yes' and then told others about my new venture. I didn't know it then, but that one email changed the trajectory of my life forever.

Next Level Collaboration has been both the most challenging and most fulfilling thing I have ever done, and might ever do. For all the sleepless nights, deadline crunches, and 'how are we ever going to do this?'

> moments, there has also been immeasurable reward in building a community of neurodivergent adults whose experiences are parallel to my own. Every day, I am driven to succeed by the younger version of myself who needed something just like Next Level Collaboration – a place where she was celebrated and could belong. The traits that caused that undiagnosed little girl to be deemed 'difficult' and 'stubborn' and many adults 'just didn't know what to do with her' eventually became the things that made her a not just a successful leader, but the first openly neurodivergent CEO of a University of Melbourne startup, which also happened to be the first social enterprise to spin out of the University of Melbourne.
>
> The world I have built for myself is wonderfully neurodivergent, but I am often acutely reminded that broader society is very neurotypically normed. Some days feel overwhelmingly demanding, but when I look in the mirror and see that young girl who never thought she could achieve anything like this, I remember what this is all about and find the strength to keep going, for her.

Both Jess and Inga discussed how discovering themselves, later in life, sparked a drive to become the mentor and create the spaces their younger selves needed. This drive to improve things for others has been a sentiment shared throughout these vignettes. Inga is, as her identity unfolds, becoming the mentor and advocate she needed, and Jess has harnessed this drive to start a neurodivergent social enterprise, becoming both a mentor and an inspiration.

THEME 4: FINDING IDENTITY THROUGH COMMUNITY AND SELF-DISCOVERY

The final theme of this chapter encompasses stories of finding identity, a theme that resonates throughout this book. The following two authors discuss how their identities have developed, and the important role that community has played within their own journeys of self-discovery.

Perseverance and Self-Preservation: Reflections on Navigating Education as a Trans Autistic Student – Michael Arhin-Acquaah (He/Him)

My education has always felt tumultuous and complicated. I fell into the trope of being an undiagnosed, neurodivergent little girl who excelled far too quickly. It was as if becoming a school refuser by thirteen was inevitable.

Like many Global Majority[1] individuals, professionals did not regard me as autistic, and I somehow evaded any formal diagnosis. Though teachers forever vouched for my brilliance, my COVID-predicted grades saw me off to university with nothing to show for myself and not much of an explanation for why.

I pressured myself to revert into the high achiever I once was and developed an obsession with my studies that superseded every aspect of my life. Spending entire semesters indoors and dedicating summers to resubmissions, my social life was minimal.

At the time, I felt incredibly uncertain of my achievements. I spent a lot of time thinking I did not belong anywhere; a small fish in an ocean full of sharks, with problems that did not seem to exist for anybody else.

Being queer, mixed race, and neurodivergent often meant suppressing or overlooking parts of myself to

[1]People in the world who do not consider themselves/are not considered to be white. This term is used in place of other minoritising terms such as 'minority ethnic', reclaiming power through the language we use to describe ourselves. https://blamuk.org/2025/08/29/language-power-and-the-global-majority/.

be palatable to others. I was desperate to provide an explanation for myself and my differences but had no clue where to start. I feared being 'othered' enough to hide my transition from my peers and lacked the bandwidth to mask enough to convince myself that I was fitting in.

I certainly relaxed following my diagnosis, which removed any doubts I had about my 'right' to call myself autistic. As every aspect of my identity created red tape and hesitance within the services I approached, it was a battle to access the correct academic and non-academic support. Once accessed, however, I was able to drag myself through my thesis year with satisfyingly good grades.

Determined to make this process easier for others, I worked with Good Thinking to publish a blog for university students packed full of resources and advice.

Later, I worked alongside the Gender Identity Research and Education Society (GIRES) and led a community engagement project to create concise and direct guidance to address the difficulties faced by trans autistic people.

Every focus group introduced me to a diverse range of individuals from across the country. Their unique stories (and unfortunately similar roadblocks) affirmed that my difficulties with accessing education was not a 'me problem', but rather a common outcome for individuals with differing presentations and needs.

Community connectedness is so important for people's wellbeing, especially when facing systems and structures that were not made for you. Looking back, I recognise how being so isolated from the experiences of other trans autistic people allowed me to internalise problems with education that predate me.

Speaking to others like me taught me that I do not need to sacrifice myself to succeed in situations that exclude me. Today, I define 'success' as when I can do my best whilst not feeling my worst – even if I must do it differently.

Finding My Way Through Tourette's: From Struggle to Scholarship – Mu-Yen Chan (He/Him)

Growing up with Tourette's Syndrome meant living in constant tension between my body and the world. The tics were never just physical – they were also emotional and social in nature. Every involuntary movement carried guilt, frustration, and shame. I would gather the pieces of myself after each breakdown, only to be shattered again without warning. Living with Tourette's was an unending cycle of breaking and rebuilding, but that rhythm, long before I understood it, forged the resilience that continues to sustain me.

When I finally learned what Tourette's Syndrome was, it brought both relief and revelation. The medical name gave me a framework to reinterpret my struggles with attention, learning, and communication. Yet, diagnosis alone could not erase the pain of misunderstanding and exclusion. During my master's studies, I turned to research as a way to make sense of these experiences – not only my own, but also those of others living with tics in Taiwan. I worked closely with Tourette people and helped establish Taiwan's first Tourette people-led support group. Listening to their stories, I realized that Tourette's was not a defect to be removed but a way of being in the world – one that called for deeper reflection on our very existence.

> This journey opened an unexpected academic path. Through phenomenological, sociological, and historical approaches, I explored how people with Tourette's experience themselves and society. The work was challenging but rewarding – it received academic recognition and was published (Chan, 2013, 2017). More importantly, it transformed my relationship to research itself: what began as a personal struggle evolved into a shared space of healing, dialogue, and understanding. That transformation marked my first real step into academia.
>
> Today, Tourette's continues to guide me on my academic journey. My early experiences of collective storytelling and community building remain the foundation of my PhD work. Through my encounter with Tourette's as a medical category, my experience of reassembling the relational formation between symptoms, the self, and society, I was able to pose the following questions: How is knowledge constructed? How is difference perceived? How do people come to see themselves through the conception of science and society, as they develop dynamic ways of understanding themselves through ongoing interactions with medical knowledge and social contexts? These questions lead me to continually reimagine the relationship between body, culture, and meaning. This has been a journey from confusion to clarity, from being a passive recipient of medicine to becoming a researcher who shapes knowledge within a group of living people.

These final two stories reflect back the theme that we might have to do things differently, but that is okay. While Micheal's story is personal, it reflects something that is important for all academics to learn and remember: that success shouldn't come at the expense of everything else. Likewise, Mu-Yen reiterates a driver that motivates many of the researchers in this book – the importance of shaping knowledge about ourselves, not merely being passive recipients.

FINAL REFLECTIONS

Despite the many challenges faced by neurodivergent academics, we belong in academia, and as Salome said, we are all needed to reimagine it. Trailblazers and mentors like Steven Kapp, Sandra Thom-Jones, Monique Botha, Robert Chapman, Nick Walker, TC Waisman, and many others have and are opening the doors and showing what openly neurodivergent leadership can be. But there are so many neurodivergent people who still feel, often rightly so, that it is not safe to be openly neurodivergent in academia (e.g. Sarchet, 2024). Those of us who are out, whether through privilege, happenstance, accident, stubbornness, a drive for advocacy or (most likely) a mixture of these things, understand that everyone's circumstances are different and not everyone can, at least for now, be open. But there are still ways to find community without being 'out'.

We ended here because finding community has been truly transformative to the editors and authors of this book. We can find connection and support through online communities, mentoring, friends outside of academia, disability groups, advocacy groups, and any other way our different brains can come up with. Despite the challenges we discussed throughout the book, knowing they are shared helps us all carry those burdens together and create the world our younger selves needed. It is our hope that you, the reader, feel this sense of community through reading this book and knowing you are not alone, regardless of your neurotype.

REFERENCES

Chan, Mu-Y. (2013). *Tourette syndrome, disease categories and personal identity in Taiwan* Master's thesis. National Tsing Hua University. https://hdl.handle.net/11296/79a3q8

Chan, Mu-Y. (2017). Disease categories and personal identity: Adult persons with Tourette Syndrome in Taiwan. *Technology, Medicine and Society*, *25*(October), 7–61. https://doi.org/10.6464/TJSSTM.201710_(25).0001

Das M., Tang, J., Ringland, K. E., & Piper, A. M. (2021). Towards accessible remote work: Understanding work-from-home practices of neurodivergent professionals. *Proceedings of the ACM on Human-Computer Interaction*, *5*(CSCW1), 183:1–183:30. https://doi.org/10.1145/3449282

Kennedy, L. J., Richdale, A. L., Gore, K. E., & Lawson, L. P. (2025). 'A menu would be sweet': A framework analysis of the disclosure and supports experiences of higher education students with neurodivergent or mental-health conditions. *Neurodiversity*, *3*, 27546330251352326. https://doi.org/10.1177/27546330251352326

Mellifont, D. (2023). *Ableist ivory towers: A narrative review informing about the lived experiences of neurodivergent staff in contemporary higher education*. https://doi.org/10.1080/09687599.2021.1965547

Milton, D. E. M. (2012). On the ontological status of autism: The 'double empathy problem'. *Disability & Society*, *27*(6), 883–887. https://doi.org/10.1080/09687599.2012.710008

Mutanana, N., Tsvere, M., & Chiweshe, M. (2020). Stigma and mental health misinterpretation of epilepsy in Zimbabwe: A qualitative study. *African Journal of Disability*, *9*(0), a719.

Ngwende, S. (2020). Perceptions and cultural beliefs about epilepsy in Sub-Saharan Africa: A scoping review. *Journal of Global Health Reports*, *4*, e2020045.

Oliver, M., & Barnes, C. (2012). *The new politics of disablement* (2nd ed.). Palgrave Macmillan.

Riordan, J., Timperley, S., O'Brien, C., Edwards, C., Murrihy, C., Harrison, M., McKay-Brown, L., & Mendus, A. (2024). Creating the conditions for inclusion: Investigating optimal physical spaces for supporting neurodivergent staff and postgraduate students.

Neurodiversity, 2, 27546330241285353. https://doi.org/10.1177/27546330241285353

Sarchet, L. N. (2024). Experiences of disabled and neurodivergent faculty in higher education: A systematic literature review. *Journal of Disability Studies in Education*. https://doi.org/10.1163/25888803-bja10032

Thorpe, D., McKinlay, M., Richards, J., Sang, K., & Stewart, M. E. (2024). The lived experience of autistic adults in employment: A systematic search and synthesis. *Autism in Adulthood*, 6(4), 495–509. https://doi.org/10.1089/aut.2022.0114

Timperley, S., Riordan, J., & Harrison, M. (2025). *"Being always visible means i'm never comfortable": An exploratory analysis of neurodivergent experiences of spaces and how they are utilised in a large Australian university*. https://doi.org/10.26188/30194923.v1

Young, I. M. (1990). *Justice and the politics of difference*. Princeton University Press.

ABOUT THE EDITORS

Dr. Sarah Timperley (she/her) is a Postdoctoral Research Fellow in the Faculty of Education at the University of Melbourne with a background in psychology, education and neurodiversity. Drawing on her professional and lived experiences of ADHD, she now co-leads the University of Melbourne Neurodiversity Project. She is passionate about improving the lives of neurodivergent people, including adults like herself, and has delivered dozens of seminars and workshops on supporting neurodivergent staff and students. Her current research focuses on neurodiversity in the workplace, including disclosure, accommodations and universal design of spaces and processes so that everyone can work to their strengths. She is also proudly queer and loves crafts and gardening.

Associate Professor Matthew Harrison (he/him) is an experienced teacher, researcher and digital creator who is an advocate for utilising technology to support social capacity building, belonging and inclusion in education. He has taught in Australia, South Korea and the United Kingdom at primary, secondary and tertiary levels. Matthew is currently a member of the University of Melbourne Faculty of Education Learning Intervention team, a project lead at the University of Melbourne Neurodiversity Project and the co-founder of Next Level Collaboration, the first neurodivergent-led social enterprise to spin out of the University of Melbourne. He was awarded the Dyason Fellowship in 2020, and the GEM Scott Teaching Fellowship and the International Society for Technology in Education 'Making IT Happen' award in 2023. Matthew has lived experience of ADHD which also informs his passion for inclusive education.

Dr. Jessica Riordan (nee Johnston: she/her) is a Postdoctoral Research Fellow in the Faculty of Education at the University of Melbourne with a passion for conducting neurodiversity-affirming research, translating research into practice and inspiring positive societal change through community-led advocacy and education. Drawing on her research background in developmental psychology and lived experience of neurodivergence, Jessica co-founded the University of Melbourne Neurodiversity Project in 2023. Her research focuses on neurodiversity-affirming education across the lifespan, psychological well-being, self-efficacy and self-determination, parenting, and the development of programmes that help to support young people and their families through key life transitions. Her outreach, advocacy and contributions in these spaces have also been acknowledged through leadership awards, such as the University of Otago Leadership Award and the University of Otago Division of Sciences Outreach Award.

ABOUT THE CONTRIBUTORS

Michael Arhin-Acquaah (he/him) is an aspiring clinical psychologist and researcher who is determined to promote autism acceptance in every sector he works in. He has been involved in service development for the NHS since his teens and has delivered a plethora of talks and presentations on autism, intersectionality and gender identity within educational and healthcare settings. Currently working alongside the Gender Identity Research and Education Society (GIRES), Michael is creating an Autism Resource Directory for trans autistic people which he hopes will support them in creating inclusive and accessible environments for themselves. He is very proud to have obtained a First Class BSc in Psychology from London South Bank University and is keen to take his education further.

Mu-Yen Chan (he/him) is a PhD student in the Department of Social Justice Education at the Ontario Institute for Studies in Education (OISE), University of Toronto. His research is situated at the intersection of disability studies and Indigenous studies. Living with Tourette's Syndrome has profoundly shaped both his research interests and methodological commitments. His earlier work explored how medical and social forms of knowledge shape experiences of difference, identity and embodiment, with particular attention to collective storytelling and community-based knowledge production. Mu-Yen co-founded Taiwan's first Tourette people–led support group, where research emerged through dialogue, shared reflection and lived experience rather than deficit-based frameworks. Before his doctoral studies, he spent five years teaching in an Indigenous community in Taiwan, an experience that continues to inform his current research, which engages Taiwanese Indigenous storytelling through interpretive methods and narrative inquiry to bring disability studies into meaningful dialogue with Indigenous studies.

Chris Edwards (he/him) is a Research Fellow at Aspect (Autism Spectrum Australia) and an Adjunct Research Fellow with the Inclusive Futures beacon at Griffith University. He serves as an Executive Committee member of the Australasian Society for Autism Research (ASfAR) and a Non-Executive Director of Empower Autism. Chris, who is autistic, has over 11 years' experience supporting the Autistic community across diverse roles. Chris completed his PhD through the Autism CRC in 2019. His research primarily focuses on education, mental health and adult experiences related to autism. Chris has received multiple awards and accolades in recognition of his significant contributions to autism research and community engagement.

Aimee Fletcher (she/her) is a recent PhD graduate from the University of Glasgow. Her PhD, titled 'Neurodivergence in Museums: Making the Cultural Heritage Sector Accessible Using Participatory Practices', was an interdisciplinary project funded by the Lord Kelvin and Adam Smith Studentship. Combining over a decade of experience working within autism charities, six years of neurodivergence-focused research with her lived experience, Aimee has contributed to various projects focused on making society more accessible for neurodivergent adults. Currently working as a Participation Coordinator at Scottish Autism promoting autistic-led decision-making and advocating for autistic voices to be heard, Aimee has been a consultant on various accessibility-related projects for different organisations including Museum Association (UK), National Library of Scotland, University of Edinburgh, The Hunterian (Glasgow) and the University of Stirling. Aimee is also on the INSAR Autistic Researcher's Committee as the Secretary and serves as a Social Media Editor for Autism in Adulthood.

Inga Koops (she/her) is an Autistic PhD candidate at the University of Southern Queensland, researching how universities can better support Autistic and neurodivergent students, staff and communities. Her PhD includes participatory research projects with Reframing Autism, an Autistic-led organisation, focusing on neurodiversity-affirming practice, intersectional experiences and systemic change. With nearly 20 years of experience in inclusive teaching and curriculum design across primary and secondary education, Inga specialises in creating accessible and supportive learning environments. She has a strong passion for fostering a culture of community and belonging for Autistic and neurodivergent people in higher education and also mentors Autistic and neurodivergent university students.

Kun-Rong Li (he/him) is a person with dyslexia from Taiwan. He holds a Master's degree in Social Welfare from National Chung Cheng University and is currently pursuing a PhD in Education at National Taiwan Normal University. He serves as the Managing Director of the Taiwan Youth with Disability Association. His research focuses on disability identity among young people, and his work is dedicated to advocating for the social conditions experienced by disabled youth while amplifying the voices of his generation.

Mario Liong (he/him) is an Associate Professor at the Department of Sociology at National Taipei University. He works in gender and sexuality studies, with particular interests in fatherhood, masculinities and emerging forms of technology-mediated intimate relationships and sexualities. His research is grounded in both qualitative and quantitative methods, often exploring how transformations in gender and sexual practices are made possible. Before arriving in Taiwan, Mario held academic positions across Hong Kong, Sweden and Japan. He is now working to bring new materialist thinking into sociological analysis of lived experiences, including his reflections on sensory processing sensitivity and academic life.

Katie Munday (they/he) is a community researcher, writer and doctoral candidate in psychology at the University of Portsmouth. Their work explores health and social care experiences of transgender Autistic adults in the United Kingdom. They are a co-founder of the Autistic Substance Use Network and have collaborated with healthcare professionals, community organisations and the NHS to create resources and training that promote more inclusive practice. Their research spans Disabled people's experiences of cancer services, Autistic adults' experiences of substance use and the intersections of gender diversity, neurodivergence and healthcare. Katie has over a decade of experience supporting marginalised young people and adults through community work, mentoring and inclusive sports. They also write creatively and academically for queer and neurodivergent platforms, contributing to wider conversations on intersectionality and social justice.

Salome Munyengerwi (she/her) is an emerging Zimbabwean advocate and researcher whose work lives at the intersection of lived experience and neurodiversity. She holds a Master of Science in Strategic Management (Chinhoyi University of Technology, Zimbabwe), Bachelor of Commerce in Business Management (Midlands State University, Zimbabwe) and Certificate in Corporate Social Responsibly (Alison). Her academic foundation thus deeply grounds a perspective rooted in caring for her epileptic mother and autistic brother, and mentoring neurodivergent teens. It was through these experiences that she realised how systems fail those who think and learn differently, and this set her on a path of advocacy. Salome is now pursuing a Doctorate to formalise this work, focusing her research on Burnout, Inclusion and Leadership, as well as supportive designs for inclusive educational settings that foster success for neurodivergent students in Zimbabwean and similar contexts. She champions a strength-based approach in framing neurodiversity and is committed to reimagining academia and education as spaces where different minds are celebrated.

Jenny Mai Phan (she/her) is a Research Assistant Professor in the Department of Bioengineering and Assistant Director of Community Engagement at the Center for Medtech Innovation at George Mason University. Her interdisciplinary research spans developmental science, behavioural endocrinology and intellectual and developmental disabilities. Dr Phan is a Vietnamese American, first-generation college graduate and late-diagnosed autistic researcher. She served as a public member in the U.S. Department of Health and Human Services' Interagency Autism Coordinating Committee from 2021 to 2024. She holds leadership positions in multiple professional organisations, including co-chairing the Diversity Committee on the Association for Behavioral and Cognitive Therapies Autism Special Interest Group and serving on the executive committee of the American Association on Intellectual and Developmental Disabilities Psychology Interest Network. Her research has been supported by the National Institutes of Health and published work in autism journals including *Autism in Adulthood* and *Journal of Autism and Developmental Disorders*.

Kathryn E. Ringland (Kate) Ringland (she/her) is an Assistant Professor at the University of California Santa Cruz, where she runs the Misfit Lab in the Computational Media Department. She received her PhD in Informatics from the University of California Irvine. Kate's areas of interest include human computer interaction, online communities, play and critical disability studies. She is interested in understanding how play facilitates and subverts the ways in which we socialise and view the world. Current work in the Misfit Lab includes exploring how technology can support disabled and neurodivergent individuals, sociality and well-being and fandom and other communities of play.

Jess Rowlings (she/her) is a qualified speech and language pathologist and co-founder/CEO of Next Level Collaboration, a social enterprise that runs strength-based programmes to support neurodivergent children in developing collaborative skills and social connection through cooperative video games. She is proudly the first openly neurodivergent CEO from a University of Melbourne spinout company. Jess also serves as an Honorary Enterprise Fellow and researcher at the University of Melbourne Faculty of Education who specialises in the design and analysis of video game–based intervention to build social capacity in neurodivergent children. Her work has included developing and running a dedicated Minecraft server to support neurodivergent girls and women. Informed by her lived experience of receiving autism and ADHD diagnoses as an adult as well as her lifelong love of games, Jess is completing her PhD investigating the experiences of neurodivergent women in gaming communities.

Ari Star (she/her) is an autistic research assistant and casual tutor with narcolepsy and dysautonomia. She completed a Bachelor of Human Sciences in Public Health before progressing into higher-degree research, undertaking a Bachelor of Philosophy. She is now completing a Master of Research investigating the role of Universal Design for Learning on neurodivergent students' university experiences. Ari is enthusiastic about bringing lived experience of disability to her work and enjoys taking part in co-designed projects with other neurodivergent researchers. Through her research and advocacy work, she aims to improve educational spaces to better anticipate and respond to the needs of neurodivergent people by listening to their preferences rather than assuming their requirements. In addition to research, Ari is a competitive powerlifter and enjoys spending her evenings at the gym with her fiancé, Jay. At the time of writing, most of her spare time is spent working on a very detailed spreadsheet for her upcoming wedding.

Sandra C. Thom-Jones (she/her), MBA, MPH, PhD, is an autistic author, artisan, academic and advocate. She is the author of *Growing in to Autism* (Melbourne University Press, 2022; 2025), *Autistics in Academia* (Cambridge University Press, 2025) and *Autistics at Work* (Melbourne University Press, 2025). Sandra worked for more than two decades in the university sector as a researcher and senior leader, most recently as Pro Vice-Chancellor, Research Impact. She now works as a consultant providing a range of services for autistic people – as well as research and consultancy services for education, employment and healthcare providers – through her website Autistic Professor. She is also an Honorary Professor at the University of Wollongong. Sandra has undertaken numerous research projects in partnership with the autistic community on the experiences of autistic people, autistic parenting, autism and ageing, autism in the media and the knowledge and attitudes towards autism in the broader community.

GLOSSARY

Academic, activist, advocate (roles)—Overlapping identities taken up by neurodivergent scholars who combine research, public engagement and community organising.
Academic assemblages—A term drawn from assemblage theory (e.g., Deleuze and Guattari) that refers to the dynamic, shifting networks of people, ideas, policies, technologies, spaces, discourses and power relations that together produce what we recognise as 'academia'.
Academic hierarchies—Formal and informal structures of power in universities (e.g. PhD student vs supervisor, lecturer vs senior management).
Academic metrics/KPIs—Quantitative performance measures (e.g. publication counts, impact factors, student evaluations) used to judge academics.
Academic precarity—Insecure employment conditions (e.g., short-term contracts, casual work, uncertain renewal).
Academic promotion—Formal advancement through academic ranks, shaped by hidden criteria and politics.
Accommodation (workplace/study)—Adjustments to tasks, environments or expectations intended to enable disabled and neurodivergent people to participate on equal terms (e.g., flexible hours, sensory-friendly spaces, extra time).
Administrative burden—The growing load of paperwork, reporting, compliance and 'business improvement' tasks expected of academics, often without training or time.
Anti-intellectualism—Wider social hostility or suspicion towards universities, expertise and research, adding external pressure to an already strained sector.
Assemblage (Deleuze and Guattari)—A concept used to understand how spaces, rules, bodies and affects come together to enable or constrain what capacities arise.
Autistic burnout—A pervasive state of exhaustion and reduced functioning experienced by autistic people after prolonged stress, masking and unmet support needs.
Autistic masking—See Masking.
Autism diagnosis (adult)—Processes by which adults are assessed and labelled as autistic, often delayed or inaccessible for women, people of colour and high achievers.

Autism research politics—Tensions over who defines autism, which models are used and whose interests research serves.

Autism in Adulthood (journal)—A key journal referenced in the book that publishes work on adult autistic experiences, often with community involvement.

Belonging (academic)—A sense of being recognised, valued and included within academic communities; often forged in neurodivergent-led or disability-affirming spaces.

Bureaucratic barriers (HR/disability services)—Complex forms, procedures and gatekeeping that make it hard to request or maintain accommodations.

Burnout (general)—Severe depletion of energy, motivation and capacity to work due to chronic stress; in the book linked to neo-liberal reforms, scarcity and invisible caring labour.

Burnout in environments shaped by scarcity—Burnout that arises where resources, time and security are chronically scarce and care is exploited rather than resourced.

Boycott Spectrum 10K—A community-led campaign challenging a large autism genetics study, highlighting consent, ethics and distrust of some research agendas.

Care (as resistance)—Using care for oneself and others (e.g., emotionally, practically, structurally) as a deliberate counter to exploitative academic cultures.

Career disruptions—Interruptions to expected academic timelines due to health, pregnancy, caregiving, burnout, visa issues or other circumstances.

Caring labour (emotional/pastoral)—Unrecognised work academics do to support students and colleagues (e.g., listening, mentoring, crisis support), vital but rarely counted in metrics.

Co-design (research)—A collaborative process where stakeholders (e.g., service users, students, community members) actively participate in designing a programme, intervention, policy, curriculum or resource.

Co-production (research)—A broader partnership approach to co-design, in which stakeholders are meaningfully involved across the entire lifecycle of a project or service (e.g., design plus implementation, delivery, evaluation, governance and dissemination).

Code-switching (cultural and neurotypical)—Shifting language, behaviour or presentation to match dominant expectations. For example, masking autistic traits and conforming to racialised norms simultaneously.

Community of practice (research)—Groups of researchers and practitioners learning with and from each other, sometimes explicitly neurodivergent-centred.

Cultural competemility—A combined stance of cultural competence and cultural humility to describe an approach to intercultural engagement that combines knowledge and skill with ongoing self-reflection and power awareness. For example, asking professionals and institutions to treat autistic people as experts in their own lives and to adjust practice accordingly.

Cultural politics of disability—Ways that disability identities are formed, valued or marginalised within particular societies, institutions and movements.

Deficit model of neurodivergence—A framework that defines neurodivergence primarily as deficits needing remediation.

Deterritorialisation (Deleuze and Guattari)—A shift away from established patterns (e.g. moving countries or roles) that destabilises old routines and opens new possibilities.

Diagnosis vs self-identification—The distinction between formally diagnosed and self-identified neurodivergent people and debates about legitimacy, access to services and research inclusion.

Disability rights movement—Social movements led by disabled people seeking access, rights and systemic change; intersecting with the neurodiversity movement.

Disclosure (of neurodivergence)—Telling others in the workplace or academy about one's neurodivergent identity, often balancing potential support against risk of discrimination.

Double empathy problem—The idea that autistic–non-autistic miscommunication is mutual and relational, not simply a deficit in autistic people.

Double masking/triple masking—Layered masking by people who navigate multiple forms of discrimination such as racism, sexism and ableism simultaneously (e.g. autistic women of colour adjusting behaviour on several fronts at once).

Early career researchers (ECRs)—Scholars in the first years after PhD, often juggling precarious employment, high expectations and steep learning curves.

Emotional dysregulation—Difficulty managing intense emotions, often intensified by sensory overload, social stress or burnout.

Emotional labour (academic)—The work of managing one's own emotions and others' feelings (e.g. students in crisis), typically unrecognised and unevenly distributed.

Empathy (autistic vs neurotypical)—Differently patterned forms of empathy, with autistic people often showing deep cognitive and affective empathy, but in ways misread by neurotypical observers.

Epistemic injustice—Harms done to people as knowers (e.g., dismissing neurodivergent or trans scholars' lived experience as biased while treating neurotypical perspectives as an objective.)

Exam-oriented education systems—School systems focused on rote learning and exam performance.

Executive function challenges—Difficulties planning, organising, initiating and switching tasks; common for autistic and ADHD academics and exacerbated by vague or shifting expectations.

Flexible work arrangements—Formal or informal adjustments to when and how work is done, including remote work.

Fulbright scholarships/fellowships—Prestigious international fellowships.

Gender diversity and neurodivergence—Intersections between trans or gender diverse identities and neurodivergence, including distinct experiences of marginalisation and healthcare barriers.

Global Majority—People who are racialised as non-white in Western contexts but collectively constitute the majority of the world's population.

Grant culture—The intense competition for limited research funding, shaping what projects are possible and who is seen as 'successful'.

Hazardous work environments (sensory)—Academic settings that involve noise, bright lights, crowds or other sensory challenges that are exhausting for neurodivergent people.

Hidden curriculum (academia)—The unwritten rules and expectations that govern success in academia, often inaccessible to those without insider mentors.
Hidden/invisible disability—Disabilities and neurodivergent conditions that are not apparent to others, frequently doubted or dismissed as excuses.
Higher education governance—Structures and practices by which universities are managed and held accountable.
Hyperfocus—Intense, sustained concentration on highly interesting topics or tasks.

Imposter syndrome—Feelings of fraudulence and self-doubt despite evidence of competence.
Inclusive teaching—Practices that intentionally design courses to meet diverse cognitive, sensory and cultural needs, reducing reliance on individual accommodations.
Infantilisation (of autistic adults)—Treating autistic adults as children (e.g., questioning their competence and authority, especially in professional or leadership roles).
Institutional betrayal—Harm caused when institutions fail to protect or support individuals who trusted them, for example, mishandling complaints or ignoring access needs.
Institutional hierarchies—See academic hierarchies.
Institutional violence (symbolic/procedural)—Non-physical harms such as stereotyping, erasure, punitive policies and constant insecurity that cumulatively damage neurodivergent staff and students.
Intersectionality—The way multiple identities (e.g. race, gender, sexuality, gender diversity, disability, class, neurodivergence) combine to shape experiences of privilege and oppression.

Lab politics—Interpersonal tensions, competition, favouritism and power struggles within research groups.
Late diagnosis—Receiving an autism, ADHD or other neurodivergent diagnosis in adulthood rather than childhood.
Learning disability—A lifelong neurodevelopmental difference that affects how a person processes, understands or applies certain types of information. It reflects variation in cognitive development and learning profiles, rather than lack of intelligence or effort.
Line of flight (Deleuze and Guattari)—Paths of transformation or escape within an assemblage. For example, a new research direction or a move to a different institution.
Lived experience (in neurodiversity research)—Knowledge gained through living neurodivergence, increasingly recognised as essential in shaping ethical and meaningful research.

Mad studies/Mad scholarship—An interdisciplinary field of scholarship and activism led primarily by people with lived experience of psychiatric diagnoses, mental distress and/or institutionalisation. It critically examines how psychiatry, mental health systems and broader social structures define, manage and often marginalise ‘madness’.
Masking (camouflaging)—Consciously or unconsciously hiding or suppressing neurodivergent traits to conform to neurotypical expectations.

Medical model of disability/autism—An approach that locates problems in individuals' bodies or brains and seeks cure or normalisation, as opposed to focusing on social barriers.
Microaggressions—Everyday slights or comments that subtly express prejudice or disbelief; often denied as 'not real' by those in power.
Misfit (disability concept)—The experience of not fitting into environments designed for other kinds of bodies and minds; can be alleviated by changing environments, not people.
Misogyny/sexism in academia—Gendered biases that shape expectations and opportunities.

Narrative and autoethnographic methods—Research approaches that use personal stories and reflective writing to explore systemic issues from the inside.
Neo-liberal university/marketisation of higher education—The transformation of universities from institutions for public good into competitive, market-driven institutions focused on profit, branding and metrics.
Neurodivergence—Perceived variations seen in cognitive, affectual and sensory functioning, differing from the majority of the general population or 'predominant neurotype'.
Neurodivergent—People with perceived variations seen in cognitive, affectual and sensory functioning, differing from the majority of the general population or 'predominant neurotype'.
Neurodiversity—The diversity of human brains and minds; also the movement arguing that neurodivergence is part of human variation, not a defect.
Neurodiversity approach(es)—An umbrella for theories and practices that respect neurodivergent people's rights, centre their perspectives and question deficit-based frameworks.
Neurodiversity-affirming research/practice—Work that values neurodivergent ways of being, focuses on reducing barriers and avoids pathologising language and goals.
Neurodiversity paradigm—A conceptual framework that understands neurodivergence within social, political and cultural contexts rather than simply as individual pathology.
Neurodivergent-led spaces—Labs, programmes, communities and social enterprises designed and governed by neurodivergent people.
Neurodivergent research communities—Loose or formal networks of neurodivergent researchers.
Neurodivergent spiky profiles—Uneven patterns of ability, where individuals may have very high skill in some areas and significant difficulty in others.
Neurotypical—People whose cognitive, affective and sensory functioning is perceived to align with the majority of the general population, or the socially constructed 'predominant neurotype'.

Open-plan offices—Shared workspaces, often without adequate sound or visual barriers.
Othering—Processes by which individuals or groups are treated as fundamentally different and lesser, often through stereotypes, exclusion or erasure.

Participatory research—Research where autistic, disabled and neurodivergent people are active partners across different stages, including sharing power with academics.

Performance management—Formal systems used to monitor and 'correct' staff performance.
Performance metrics (academia)—See Academic metrics/KPIs.
PhD supervisor/supervisory team—The person or people formally responsible for shepherding a PhD student through their PhD studies, including providing information, support and guidance. Supervisors are usually also responsible for communicating progress and performance with the candidate and university.
PhD transitions (student to academic)—The complex move from doctoral study to academic employment, often involving hidden expectations, informal networks and narrow job markets.
Physical workspace design—The arrangement and sensory qualities of offices, classrooms and informal spaces, and their impact on neurodivergent comfort and productivity.
Promotion advice (gendered/neurotypical)—Career guidance that assumes neurotypical and male life patterns, often ill-suited to neurodivergent or caregiving academics.

Queer methodologies—Research approaches grounded in queer theory and lived experience that challenge normative assumptions and embrace fluidity and multiplicity.
Quiet spaces/low impact sensory rooms—Intentionally designed university spaces with reduced sensory input, providing refuge for neurodivergent students and staff.

Reasonable adjustments/accommodations—See Accommodation (workplace/study).
Re-diagnosis/changing diagnostic labels—Reassessment of prior diagnoses (e.g. 'Asperger's', 'ASD Level 2') in light of evolving criteria and self-understanding.
Reflexivity (researcher positionality)—Researchers' critical reflection on how their identities and experiences shape their work, interactions and interpretations.
Remote/hybrid work—Working some or all of the time from home.

Scarcity (institutional)—Chronic lack of resources, staff, time and security, creating competition and making care work especially precarious.
Self-advocacy (neurodivergent)—Speaking up about one's needs, rights and boundaries in academic and workplace contexts.
Self-care (for neurodivergent people)—Essential practices that sustain body and mind (e.g., rest, boundaries, sensory regulation, connection).
Sensory overload—Being overwhelmed by sensory input (e.g., noise, light, movement, smell), causing distress and reduced functioning.
Sensory processing sensitivity (SPS)/Highly Sensitive Person (HSP)—A temperament trait involving heightened sensitivity, deep processing and strong emotional responses to stimuli.
Side quests (academic)—Additional roles and projects outside of the requirements of a thesis or academic position (e.g., committees, outreach, mentoring).
Social dynamics (department/lab)—Patterns of inclusion, exclusion, conflict and alliance in academic teams that shape who feels safe and supported.
Social justice in higher education—Commitment to equity, access and structural change.
Social model of disability—The view that disability arises from social and environmental barriers rather than individual deficit.

Specific learning difficulties (SpLDs)—Neurodevelopmental differences that affect particular areas of learning, such as reading, writing, mathematics, motor coordination or processing speed (e.g., dyslexia, dyscalculia, dysgraphia).
Stigma (autism/neurodivergence)—Negative stereotypes and discrimination that shape how neurodivergent people are treated and how they see themselves.
Student evaluations of teaching (SETs)—Student feedback mechanisms that can influence job security and promotion.

Temporalities of academia (pace and timing)—The rhythms of semesters, deadlines, contracts and career stages that may clash with neurodivergent needs and caregiving.
Tourette's Syndrome—A neurotype with motor and vocal tics; here explored as a lived experience shaping identity and scholarship.
Trans and gender diverse (TGD) neurodivergent experiences—Lived realities of people who are both trans/gender diverse and neurodivergent.
Trauma and academia—Cumulative impact of bullying, exclusion, institutional betrayal and overwork on nervous systems and mental health.

Universal Design/Universal Design for Learning (UDL)—Designing environments and curricula from the outset to be accessible and flexible for diverse bodies and minds.
Unwritten rules (of academia)—See Hidden curriculum (academia).

Visibility (hypervisibility and invisibility)—Being always noticed yet not understood (hypervisible), or overlooked and unacknowledged (invisible).
Vignettes (personal)—Short, self-contained narrative pieces used to illustrate lived experience.

Whiteness and autism research—The dominance of white perspectives and samples in autism studies, leading to misrecognition and marginalisation of Global Majority autistic people.
Work–life boundary difficulties—Struggles keeping work from consuming personal time, especially when academic culture normalises long hours and overcommitment.
Worker–carer role conflict—Tensions between academic responsibilities and caring roles, intensified when institutional expectations ignore caregiving realities.

INDEX

www.ingramcontent.com/pod-product-compliance
Lightning Source LLC
LaVergne TN
LVHW011451220826
846271LV00026B/206